GUIDE TO THE ALLEGHENY FRONT TRAIL

THIRD EDITION

BEN CRAMER

an imprint of Sunbury Press, Inc.
Mechanicsburg, PA USA

an imprint of Sunbury Press, Inc.
Mechanicsburg, PA USA

Copyright © 2025 by Ben Cramer.
Cover Copyright © 2025 by Sunbury Press, Inc.

Sunbury Press supports copyright. Copyright fuels creativity, encourages diverse voices, promotes free speech, and creates a vibrant culture. Thank you for buying an authorized edition of this book and for complying with copyright laws. Except for the quotation of short passages for the purpose of criticism and review, no part of this publication may be reproduced, scanned, or distributed in any form without permission. You are supporting writers and allowing Sunbury Press to continue to publish books for every reader. For information contact Sunbury Press, Inc., Subsidiary Rights Dept., PO Box 548, Boiling Springs, PA 17007 USA or legal@sunburypress.com.

For information about special discounts for bulk purchases, please contact Sunbury Press Orders Dept. at (855) 338-8359 or orders@sunburypress.com.

To request one of our authors for speaking engagements or book signings, please contact Sunbury Press Publicity Dept. at publicity@sunburypress.com.

FIRST CATAMOUNT PRESS EDITION: April 2025

Set in Adobe Garamond | Interior design by Crystal Devine | Cover by Lawrence Knorr | Edited by Debra Reynolds. All photos by the author.

Publisher's Cataloging-in-Publication Data
Names: Cramer, Ben, author.
Title: Guide to the Allegheny Front Trail / Ben Cramer.
Description: First trade paperback edition. | Mechanicsburg, PA : Catamount Press, 2025.
Summary: A point-by-point guide to the Allegheny Front Trail, a 42-mile loop trail in Centre County, Pennsylvania that travels through Moshannon State Forest and Black Moshannon State Park. Guides to the connecting Moss-Hanna Trail, Shingle Mill Trail, and Rock Run Trails System are included.
Identifiers: ISBN : 979-8-88819-276-4 (softcover).
Subjects: SPORTS & RECREATION / Hiking | TRAVEL / Northeast / Middle Atlantic (NJ, NJ, PA) | NATURE / Regional.

Designed in the USA
0 1 1 2 3 5 8 13 21 34 55

For the Love of Books!

Cover: Ralph's Majestic Vista, from the southeastern section of the Allegheny Front Trail.

TABLE OF CONTENTS

Author's Note	vii
Acknowledgments	ix
About the Allegheny Front Trail System	1
Access and Logistics	12
Guide to the Allegheny Front Trail	20
Guide to the Moss-Hanne Trail	59
Guide to the Shingle Mill Trail	67
Guide to the Rock Run Trails System	72
About the Author	83
Mapping Information	84

AUTHOR'S NOTE

This guidebook accurately reflects measurements and observations that were made along the Allegheny Front Trail and its affiliated trails. The main loop of the Allegheny Front Trail was fully mapped and measured by the author in Spring 2023, and the same was done for the Moss-Hanne Trail, Shingle Mill Trail, and Rock Run Trails System in Spring 2024.

All efforts have been made to ensure accuracy in descriptions of the features and logistics of the trail, and the distances involved. However, conditions in the natural world are constantly changing. Fallen trees, flash floods, forestry practices, human developments, and myriad other phenomena often necessitate the rerouting of hiking trails and can damage infrastructure such as footbridges. Changes in the route or condition of the trail may be completed by the Pennsylvania Department of Conservation and Natural Resources, Keystone Trails Association, or other volunteers after this guide is published.

All persons using this guide do so at their own risk, and this guide should not be used without adequate maps and other common-sense precautions, which should be practiced by all outdoorspersons. The author, publisher, and trail workers/volunteers disclaim any and all liability for trail conditions, hazards, incidents encountered by hikers, and inaccuracies in this guide that may be the result of future developments. Also, the reader should follow this guide's recommendations for water sources and camping locations at his/her own risk. Please contact the author about any changes encountered along the trail that should be included in future editions of this guide.

ACKNOWLEDGMENTS

The joy of hiking in Pennsylvania would not be possible without the contributions of volunteer trail builders, maintainers, and observers. Hikers and backpackers may not even notice the valuable work of these volunteers, but they would surely notice if all that hard work was no longer being performed. Thanks to all the trail club volunteers and state forest employees in Pennsylvania who make our trails so enjoyable.

I have written three editions of the *Guide to the Allegheny Front Trail*, and all were based on full measuring and mapping projects dating back to 2006. All these projects benefited greatly from the logistical support and companionship offered by various friends and colleagues at different times, and I will thank everyone here: Chalandra Bryant, Gary Thornbloom, Dave Coleman, the Johnson family (Kyle, Heidi, and Ron), the Kotala family (Helena, Alice, and Stan), Ronn Brourman, Joe Banks, Bill and Judy Tanner, Joe and Wendy Selego, and Greg Tothero. Extra special thanks to Ralph Seeley for not just serving as the inspiration for the AFT itself, but also for decades of actively supporting Central Pennsylvania's hikers. Ralph provided significant historical knowledge that has enhanced all three editions of this guide.

Meanwhile, I recorded recent changes to the Allegheny Front Trail when leading group hikes for Keystone Trails Association in 2021 through 2023, and I would like to thank the staff members who organized those trips in which I took advantage of their logistical support while showing off the trial to some new fans. This includes Casey Schneck, Brook Lenker, and Joe Neville. Thanks also to Lawrence Knorr and Katie Cressman of Sunbury Press for their interest in publishing a new series of guidebooks for Pennsylvania hiking trails.

ABOUT THE ALLEGHENY FRONT TRAIL SYSTEM

INTRODUCTION

The Allegheny Front Trail (AFT) is a 41.86-mile-long loop trail in Moshannon State Forest in western Centre County, Pennsylvania, that roughly circles Black Moshannon State Park. Except for a short distance within the state park boundaries, the entire length of the AFT is within the state forest. The nearest town is Philipsburg, about 8 miles to the west, while State College and Penn State University are about 20 miles to the southeast.

Trail founder Ralph Seeley has written extensively on the development of the AFT and other nearby trails, as well as the history of the surrounding region going back to pioneer days. To avoid repetition, the author of this guidebook wishes to direct interested persons to the source, to get historical information from the acknowledged expert in the field. Seeley's book *Greate Buffaloe Swamp* is a fascinating history of the Moshannon region with descriptions of many of its hiking trails. Seeley also published a condensed version titled *Foot Trails of the Moshannon and Southern Elk State Forests* (4th edition, 2014).

Whereas this guidebook contains a greater amount of detail for the hiker on the Allegheny Front Trail, Seeley's *Foot Trails of the Moshannon and Southern Elk State Forests* has been consulted for more historical and ecological information. Wherever relevant, this guide features page numbers next to the citation [Seeley] for readers who wish to find more information on some of the manmade and natural features encountered along the AFT.

NOTES ON THE THIRD EDITION

Previous editions of this guidebook described the Allegheny Front Trail as 41.75 miles long. The previous edition was published in 2014 and was based on measurements and observations recorded that year.

In the late 2010s, some segments of the AFT were altered by trail maintainers to get around obstacles or to access new footbridges, and there was a significant relocation that replaced about one mile of the old trail near Shirks Road. The author completed a new measurement in 2023 for this edition of the guidebook, and the total length of the trail has increased slightly to 41.86 miles.

This edition includes a guide to the nearby Shingle Mill Trail, which was included in the previous edition and remeasured in 2024. This edition adds new chapters on the Moss-Hanne Trail and Rock Run Trails System, which the author fully measured and mapped in 2024. While these "affiliated" trails are often described as spurs of the AFT, each is unique and worth discovering in its own right.

THE HIKING LANDSCAPE

On a topographic map of Pennsylvania, the Allegheny Front is a very dramatic feature. This abrupt uprising in the landscape marks the boundary between the parallel valleys and sharp-backed ridges of the aptly named

Ridge and Valley Province to the south and east, and the high jumbled hills of the Allegheny Plateau to the north and west. Passengers on commuter flights traveling eastbound toward State College will see a rolling landscape plunging dramatically into Bald Eagle Valley, while pilots flying in the other direction face a steep forested wall of dimensions seen in few other places east of the Mississippi.

The Allegheny Front, which is a key component of the Appalachian Mountain system, comes northeast-bound out of Maryland, looms over Altoona, passes one valley to the west of State College, and then swings to the east past Lock Haven and Williamsport before merging into the Endless Mountains region in Sullivan County. The Allegheny Front constitutes a major change in elevation and geology, and a boundary between ecosystems and forest types.

In this age of superhighways that leap tall mountains in a single bound, it's hard to imagine that the Allegheny Front was once a significant barrier to the westward expansion of America. Pioneers had to squeeze through the razor-thin valleys of the Susquehanna and Juniata Rivers or go all the way around to New York or Maryland. Railroads didn't conquer the Front until Altoona's Horseshoe Curve was constructed in the 1850s, and to this day few major roads tackle the Front without serious grades and dangerous curves.

The Allegheny Front Trail follows its namesake Front for only a short distance, though it visits many different ecosystems and landscapes in and near Black Moshannon State Park. The AFT was built in the late 1990s with the express purpose of visiting both the park and the vistas along the Front. The trail was constructed to complement the Rock Run Trails System (RRTS), which had been built in the early 1980s for cross-country skiers. The leading inspiration for the RRTS, veteran Pennsylvania trail maintainer and historian Ralph Seeley, also supervised the exploration and construction of the Allegheny Front Trail. Utilizing portions of the existing RRTS, the Moss-Hanne Trail in Black Moshannon State Park, old road and railroad grades in Moshannon State Forest, and some newly constructed trail segments, the AFT was completed in the late 1990s.

DAY HIKES AND BACKPACKING TRIPS

Thanks to its loop layout and many access points, the Allegheny Front Trail is great for both day hikes and extended backpacking trips. For the planning of hikes, this guide describes the entire AFT loop in a clockwise fashion, starting at the parking lot shared with the Rock Run Trails System (see the *Access and Logistics* chapter below for details).

Both the starting point and direction of the measurements in this guide were completely arbitrary decisions. The hiker can start where desired and can hike in either direction. Just note that when hiking the AFT loop in a counter-clockwise direction, all features will be mirror images of those described in this guide. For example, uphill becomes downhill, left turns become right turns, and the like. Also, there is no need to feel constrained by the four "sections" of the AFT loop denoted in this guide, which were also created arbitrarily for readability and planning purposes.

The AFT is one of the most accessible trails in Pennsylvania for extended backpacking trips, and it is especially well-suited for beginners. The AFT is rarely a significant distance from a road, including the paved Rattlesnake Pike (PA Route 504) and Beaver Road. The trail is not especially rugged, except for the rocky sections along the edge of the Allegheny Front in the southeastern portion of the trail. There are also few significant climbs along the AFT, with the notable exception of the extended climb away from Moshannon Creek in the northwestern corner of the trail, plus some intermediate climbs away from Six Mile Run and Benner Run.

Otherwise, the AFT mostly features moderate to gentle terrain, and makes up for its lack of ruggedness with delightful scenery and aesthetic variety. Experienced backpackers may be able to complete the entire AFT in four days or less. Beginners, or those who prefer a more relaxed pace, can expect to complete the trail in four to six days.

For day hikers of all levels of ability, your present author strongly recommends hikes of the out-and-back variety. Start at one of the more accessible parking spots, follow the trail for a certain distance, then turn around and return to your car. Not only can you tell your friends that you have completed that section of the trail twice, but this is a useful technique for piecing together a series of day hikes into a complete transit of a long-distance trail. Besides, hikers are often surprised by how much scenery they can miss by following a trail in only one direction.

Other nearby trails are also included in this guide. The Moss-Hanne Trail traverses much of Black Moshannon State Park, visits many unique wetland ecosystems, and joins the southern segment of the AFT. The Shingle Mill Trail, a very scenic footpath that follows Black Moshannon Creek north from the state park, connects with the northern section of the AFT. Either of those can be utilized for longer backpacking trips; but should also be considered for enjoyable day hikes as well. Meanwhile, the Rock Run Trails System is connected to the northeastern portions of the AFT and offers its own loop network that is ideal for a lengthy day hike or a beginner's backpacking trip.

CAMPING

Hikers can camp in the backcountry of Moshannon State Forest with supplies that they carry in themselves. The Allegheny Front Trail is a good trail for practicing your overnight skills and assessing your ability to carry the heavy pack needed for tougher projects in the future. Consider taking the opportunity to park at a trailhead and walk a relatively short distance to a camping spot.

In Pennsylvania state forest terminology, backcountry camping comes in two flavors: car camping (where you can park directly at a campsite) and primitive camping (on foot with a backpack). There are no car camping sites adjacent to the AFT. Primitive camping is permitted anywhere in state forest lands, with some restrictions as discussed below. This applies to most of the AFT and the Shingle Mill Trail, and all of the Rock Run Trails System.

Note that primitive camping is prohibited within the boundaries of Black Moshannon State Park. This applies to a few miles of the southern segment of the AFT, the southern end of the Shingle Mill Trail, and all of the Moss-Hanne Trail. Within the state park, camping is available at the organized campgrounds for the prevailing nightly fee.

In Moshannon State Forest, statewide camping rules apply. The Pennsylvania Department of Conservation and Natural Resources (DCNR) maintains rules and regulations for primitive camping on state forest lands. DCNR utilizes camping permits, which are mostly used for recordkeeping and safety purposes, and are free of charge at the time of this writing. Also, at the time of writing, primitive backpackers are not required to apply for a camping permit except if any of the following conditions apply:

- An emergency point of contact is desired.
- You plan to stay at the same site for more than one night.
- A campfire is planned during the spring or fall fire seasons.
- You are group camping (more than 10 people.)

This process is designed to control the damage that could result from large numbers of campers in sensitive areas. Note that camping permits are not issued to persons under 18. To apply for a camping permit, visit the DCNR website at www.dcnr.pa.gov. The site will direct you to navigate to the page for the applicable state forest district office where you will then find the necessary contact information and instructions.

Important Primitive Camping Rules: DCNR maintains many rules for primitive camping in the state forests. Some of these will seem like common sense to experienced outdoorspersons, but others are unique to Pennsylvania conditions. For the most up-to-date rules, see the official state document "Primitive Camping in State Forests and Parks" which can also be found at the DCNR website.

Backpackers in Pennsylvania should observe the following important rules, among others:

- Carry out all trash. Repeat: ALL trash.
- Choose a spot that does not require the clearing of vegetation.
- Stay at least 100 feet away from any flowing stream or open water source.
- Do not wash clothes, dishes, or campsite equipment directly in a stream or spring. Collect water in a container and do your washing away from the source, and then dispose of the wastewater at least 200 feet from the source.

- Whenever possible, camp at least 25 feet from the trail, and preferably out of sight of the trail.
- Dispose of human waste by burying it in a hole at least 6 inches deep. Bring a camp trowel or small shovel for this purpose. Disposal sites should be at least 200 feet from water sources.
- Do not build a campfire during the dry seasons of spring and fall, or during other periods of abnormally high fire danger. At other times, small campfires are permitted. At previously unused campsites, construct a fire ring with nearby rocks to prevent the flames from spreading, and scatter the ring before leaving the site.
- Do not chop down live trees for firewood. Only use downed and dead wood near your campsite. Power saws are not permitted except with prior permission from the relevant state forest office.

Also, though it is not a state forest rule, beware of camping in or near the copses of rhododendron and mountain laurel that are common in Pennsylvania. These plants are flammable and may also provide cover for disagreeable animals.

Camping Locations Mentioned in This Guide: The author has made an effort to point out potential primitive camping spots along the trail, with selections being made for variety and the potential for pleasant backpacking experiences. However, not all these sites may fully comply with the above rules. Some areas within larger sites listed in this guide may not be 100 feet from a water source or 25 feet from the trail. The hiker will also notice many existing campsites created by previous backpackers, which may not comply with either of those strictures. The mention of such sites in this guide should not be considered an endorsement of the possibly illegal activities of previous backpackers.

Many of the possible campsites mentioned in this guide are near streams and springs, and to follow the state forest rules you would have to find a spot along the edge of such an area that is sufficiently removed from the water. All backpackers are strongly advised to follow the DCNR's primitive camping rules, which will ensure that future backpackers will not be deprived of the opportunity. Those using this guide will camp at the described spots at their own risk.

WATER

In this age of acid rain and bacterial pathogens, all water sources encountered in the wild should be viewed with suspicion. Giardia, a waterborne bacterium that causes the gastro-intestinal illness giardiasis, has been found in mountain streams throughout Pennsylvania, resulting in many a sick hiker. While experienced outdoorspersons might be comfortable drinking wild water, no hiking guide (including this one) will recommend doing so, and such actions will be taken at your own risk.

Water found along the trail should be treated with iodine capsules or submicron filters, which can be found at sports stores and outfitters. This is the recommended strategy for backpackers. The old-school method of purifying water by boiling it at a campfire is a tedious chore that is usually not worth the effort, even when boiling is actually achieved via a small wood fire. Day hikers should have little difficulty simply packing up the water they will need at home before embarking on their day trips.

Water Sources Listed in This Guide: As of 2024, the present author has completed the Allegheny Front Trail nine times during various seasons of the year and has made an effort in this guide to describe the quality and seasonality of the water sources encountered along the trail. However, the user of this guide will consume any water found along the trail at his/her own risk. As a general rule, water found in muddy spots, seep springs, and backwaters along the sides of flowing streams should be avoided. Also, water from larger creeks should be avoided because wide waterways, by definition, have collected water from many tributaries and low-lying areas, increasing the chances of pollution. Along the AFT, avoid drinking water from "Red" Moshannon Creek (which has its own unique dangers, as will be described later in this guide), Black Moshannon Creek, Black Moshannon Lake, and Six Mile Run.

This guide describes the suspected water quality (in the experienced hiker's estimation) of the many springs and small streams encountered along the trails discussed. These readings were *not* determined scientifically, should not be taken as any type of recommendation to drink the water, and should be considered loose guidelines only. Water sources listed here as poor or not suitable should be avoided under all circumstances.

Sources described as questionable could possibly be consumed by the desperate, or hikers with high-quality filters. Sources described as acceptable or better in this guide can be consumed by any hiker with store-bought filtering equipment.

A final note on water sources described in this guide: If you visit the trails during an especially dry period, beware that the flow and quality of springs and streams as described in this guide may be reduced. In fact, some may not even be flowing by the time you reach them. Wherever possible, efforts have been made to determine the quality of water sources during various seasons.

WILDLIFE

Moshannon State Forest features the wildlife that is typical for forested areas of Central Pennsylvania. Deer are very prevalent in the region, as are smaller forest denizens such as chipmunks, squirrels, mice, and rabbits. Areas of forest that have been over-browsed by deer are very common along the AFT. Some areas, most notably Wolf Rocks, are used by deer and other animals so much that hikers may wish to pass through quickly because of voluminous droppings. However, deer are almost always harmless and will typically flee from human contact.

Birdwatchers along the AFT may be treated to sightings of rare pileated woodpeckers, plus golden eagles and even bald eagles, all of which have been spotted in the area by the author. Rare sightings of fishers (larger relatives of weasels and ferrets) and bobcats have also been reported in the area. Meanwhile, the hiker may hear reports of mountain lions—reports that are on the increase in Central Pennsylvania. For the time being such reports should be treated with skepticism, though local nature lovers can hope that this majestic animal will reclaim its ancestral homeland.

In any case, large predators are not a serious concern for hikers on the AFT. Black bears are fairly common in this region of Central Pennsylvania but are rare in the immediate area along the AFT. Black bears tend to flee from humans long before they are seen, thanks to their remarkable sense of smell. A hiker should consider it great luck to even see one. Bears should not be provoked and certainly should not be fed, which increases the chances of their behavior changing abruptly from aloof to aggressive. There is a small chance of bears harassing untended campsites, so take precautions. Porcupines and coyotes are also common in the area, and these scavengers have also been known to disturb untended campsites. However, both of these animals are quite skittish and are highly unlikely to confront humans directly.

The only truly dangerous animal in this area is the eastern timber rattlesnake. The author has seen specimens along the AFT several times over the years. This snake prefers open areas for sunning and rocky outcrops for building dens. The snake is venomous, but its bites are typically not fatal to healthy humans, with only a medium-strength temporary illness resulting for most people. (However, some people are highly allergic to the venom, leading to a more serious illness, and are probably unaware of their allergy until it is too late. Also, extra vigilance should be exercised for one's smaller hiking companions, such as dogs and young children.)

If bitten by a rattlesnake along the trail, do not panic. Return to your car quickly but in a level-headed manner and seek medical attention as soon as possible. Contrary to popular opinion, rattlesnakes rarely attack humans, but rather defend themselves when provoked. In a telling reflection of human nature, upwards of 80% of snakebite victims anywhere in the world are bitten on their hands and arms, after stupidly trying to pick up the snake. In the rare event that you encounter an eastern timber rattlesnake, retreat sensibly, leave it alone, and consider yourself lucky to have seen this unique creature in its natural habitat.

A different problem arises from insects. Mosquitoes and similar pests are ubiquitous in the region, as are ticks. Lyme Disease and related tick-borne illnesses have been reported in the area, and encounters with ticks (only a few of which actually carry the diseases) are on the rise. High-quality insect repellent is crucial on Pennsylvania hiking trails during all seasons except the deepest parts of winter.

A NOTE ON HUNTING

Hunting is permitted in most of Moshannon State Forest, including the areas traversed by the trails described in this guide. The author and the associated trail maintainers and state forest personnel disavow all responsibility for the danger in which hikers may place themselves when hunters are present. Avoid hiking in state forest areas during the big game hunting seasons in the fall and early winter. If necessary, inquire with state forest personnel beforehand to learn which areas of the forest attract the most hunters. The Pennsylvania Game Commission also manages hunting seasons for many types of small game throughout the rest of the year, though these seasons present little risk for the hiker. Nevertheless, anyone hiking in areas known to be frequented by hunters is strongly advised to wear at least one prominent piece of safety orange clothing for visibility.

ACCESS AND LOGISTICS

TRAIL MEASUREMENTS

The author personally measured and mapped the Allegheny Front Trail and the affiliated trails described in this book. Please accept the figures herein as official until the next volunteer comes along to measure the trails again.

The trails were all measured non-electronically with a measuring wheel. The type of wheel used for this book is pushed along the ground in front of the hiker, and records the distance covered in feet. Those readings are shown in the MI columns in this guide. The mileage readings were converted to metric via the simple formula of 1 kilometer=0.621 mile; the results are shown in the KM columns.

While the trails were measured in the old-school fashion, the maps in this book were created from GPS data. The author used a Garmin Oregon 450 handheld GPS device and carefully corrected the resulting data to achieve route depictions as close to reality as possible. This raw data was loaded into mapping software to create the maps. A small map of the trail system and instructions for accessing a larger map can be found at the end of this book.

Meanwhile, an excellent small-scale color map of the AFT and the affiliated trails, and nearby state park/state forest lands, can be obtained upon request from Black Moshannon State Park or Moshannon State Forest. (Note that small-scale corresponds to greater detail.) The route of the AFT is also visible on the larger-scale (less detailed) public use map for Moshannon State Forest.

BLAZES AND TRAIL CHARACTERISTICS

Most state forest hiking trails in Pennsylvania are marked with orange blazes. In an ill-advised decision in 2009, forestry officials implemented a change to the blazing on the Allegheny Front Trail after designating some portions as "multi-use" for mountain bikers and horseback riders. This has resulted in a confusing mix of blaze colors on the AFT.

As of this writing, most of the AFT is marked with yellow blazes, while some segments that have been designated as multi-use now carry blazes that are yellow and red. (Red is the official color for multi-use trails.) This has created unnecessary confusion for long-distance hikers, because affiliated trails that connect with the AFT—including the Shingle Mill Trail, the Moss-Hanne Trail, and some short access trails to parking areas—were previously blazed with different colors but are now also blazed yellow or yellow/red. The AFT hiker must now exercise extra diligence at trial junctions, while trying not to be confused when the AFT's blazes switch from merely yellow to yellow and red (and vice-versa).

In any event, the blazes are plentiful and easy to follow, except for a few problematic areas that are described in this guide. Sharp turns are usually denoted by double blazes and occasionally arrows. The rectangular blazes are typically painted on trees alongside the trail and are usually visible from a comfortable distance. In some treeless spots, poles have been secured in the ground to bear the blazes. Blazes are also occasionally on rocks underfoot. Note that for the segment of the AFT that shares a path with the Rock Run Trails System, the hiker will follow both the yellow blazes of the AFT and the blue blazes of the RRTS.

IMPORTANT INFORMATION ON AFT TRAIL SIGNS

The Allegheny Front Trail and its affiliated trails are posted with very attractive and professional signs directing hikers to points of interest, with distances included. These signs utilize sturdy brown posts with manufactured placards for the text and distances. These signs were constructed in the period shortly after the AFT was completed in the late 1990s, and the measurements are based on electronic map readings of the terrain traversed by the trail. Such technology was quite primitive at the time, as can be seen in the information on these signs.

The accuracy of the posted measurements quickly came under suspicion from experienced hikers. Tellingly, the book *50 Hikes in Central*

Pennsylvania by the late Tom Thwaites features four different day hikes that utilize various portions of the AFT, and his own readings made with a measuring wheel differ considerably from the distances on the trail signs. For example, Thwaites measured the distance from Rattlesnake Pike south to Underwood Road as 3.8 miles, but the AFT trail signs list this distance as 3.3 miles. This is a 15% discrepancy, which is considerable for hikers trying to plan a trip.

Despite the professionalism of these modern AFT trail signs, the hiking distances denoted on them are severely inaccurate and must be disregarded by the hiker. The distances in question were still present on the signs at the time of this writing, and corrections are remotely possible in the future but unlikely.

As described above, the present author surveyed the entire AFT and its affiliated trails with a measuring wheel. For the sections of the trail that were also measured in the same fashion by Tom Thwaites, the author's readings correspond with Thwaites' measurements precisely. All of the distances listed on the trail signs were found to be inaccurate to varying degrees, and some were significantly so.

This is not enough evidence to declare that a measuring wheel is always accurate. However, a statistician would deem the wheel to be reliable because of the agreement between the readings of Thwaites and the present author. This guide to the AFT is based exclusively on the measuring wheel readings, and the figures on the trail signs are not mentioned any further in the trail description.

PARKING

Parking spots for the Allegheny Front Trail and its affiliated trails are numerous and convenient (except for the extreme northeastern corner of the network). Black Moshannon State Park offers direct access to the Moss-Hanne and Shingle Mill Trails, while the AFT crosses PA Route 504 twice. Some other nearby roads provide access as well.

ALLEGHENY FRONT TRAIL

These access points are listed clockwise from the starting point used in this guide.

AFT/ROCK RUN TRAILS SYSTEM TRAILHEAD
GPS LOCATION: N40° 55.016' W77° 58.617'

This is the lot used as the starting point for this guide. The lot provides ample parking for many cars and is located at the corner of Tram Road and Rattlesnake Pike (PA Route 504). Reach the lot by following PA 504 for 4.5 miles east of the intersection with Beaver Road in the center of Black Moshannon State Park, or 7.1 miles west of old US 220 (currently known as Alternate 220) at Unionville.

UNDERWOOD ROAD
GPS LOCATION: N40° 53.599' W78° 00.101'

Parking for a few cars is available at the AFT crossing of this unpaved road, at the 3.81 mi point on the trail. The crossing is 1.3 miles northeast of Beaver Road, and 2.0 miles southwest of PA 504. The crossing can be found around a curve just to the south of Underwood Road's intersection with North Run Road. Underwood Road is mostly wide and well-maintained and can be traversed by most vehicles. However, beware of a lack of snowplowing and other maintenance during the winter.

BEAVER ROAD AND STRAWBAND BEAVER ROAD
GPS LOCATION: N40° 53.297' W78° 02.333'

A short access trail leads from this ample parking lot to the AFT at its 6.30 mi point. The lot is a short distance to the south of the AFT's crossing of Beaver Road. To reach this spot by car, take Beaver Road south for 2.1 miles from PA 504 in the center of the state park.

The yellow/red-blazed access trail begins in a corner of the parking lot, at a sign denoting the Allegheny Front Trail and the Moss-Hanne Trail. The trail passes through a brief wooded buffer, crosses Beaver Road (watch carefully for traffic), then bears left and proceeds through a pretty area of evergreens. The access trail is 0.19 mi (0.31 km) long.

This access trail ends at a junction that illustrates the confusing nature of the blaze color scheme for the AFT and affiliated trails, because in this area the access trail and the AFT are both blazed yellow/red. The post sign at the trail junction also contains an error at the time of this writing, as the trail to the left (west) is not the Moss-Hanne Trail. In fact, the Allegheny Front Trail is to the left as well as to the right.

SHIRKS AND DUG ROADS

GPS LOCATION: N40° 52.849' W78° 03.869'

From the intersection of these two dirt roads, a spur trail provides easy access to the AFT. A small parking lot that can hold about five vehicles can be found at this corner. To reach the corner of Shirks Road and Dug Road, take Strawband Beaver Road westbound away from Beaver Road for 0.3 mile, then turn right on Shirks Road. Continue westbound on Shirks Road for another 1.2 miles, and the lot is just after the encounter with Dug Road on the left.

From the parking lot, the unblazed access trail begins across the road at a post sign. The trail almost immediately bears left on an old woods lane, which leads easily to the AFT at a signed junction at its 9.18 mi point. The total distance of this access trail is 0.15 mi (0.24 km). Note that Shirks Road may not be passable for all vehicles in the winter.

SHIRKS ROAD

GPS LOCATION: N40° 52.721' W78° 04.610'

To reach this spot, travel to the lot described in the previous entry and continue westbound on Shirks Road for an additional 0.7 mile. Parking for one or two vehicles is available at a flat spot on the left side of the road, which the AFT briefly follows in this area. The parking spot is across from Lucky Ridge Camp and just after the road bridge over Black Moshannon Creek, at the trail's 10.00 mi point. Do not park in the camp's driveway or yard. Note that Shirks Road may not be passable for all vehicles in the winter, while the grass at the parking spot might get overgrown because we need volunteers to keep it clear.

CLAY MINE ROAD (adjacent to Six Mile Run Road)

GPS LOCATION: N40° 53.072' W78° 07.008'

Parking for a few vehicles is available at several points along this road, which the AFT follows for a short distance from Six Mile Run Road to the creek of the same name. This is at and around the trail's 18.53 mi point. Do not park in the driveway or yard of the hunting camp next to the road bridge. From PA 504, drive south on Six Mile Run Road 2.0 miles, then turn left (east) on Clay Mine Road. Follow that road downhill for a short distance. This access point is not recommended in winter, except for sturdier vehicles.

WEST CROSSING OF RATTLESNAKE PIKE

GPS LOCATION: N40° 54.537' W78° 06.251'

The AFT crosses Rattlesnake Pike (PA Route 504) a second time, 2.6 miles west of the "beach" at the center of Black Moshannon State Park, near the road bridge over Six Mile Run. This is at the 21.74 mi point on the trail. On the other side of the bridge from the AFT crossing is a staggered intersection with Six Mile Run Road, and both corners feature gravel areas that provide parking for several vehicles.

MEYERS RUN ROAD

GPS LOCATION: N40° 57.105' W78° 03.283'

Parking for two or three vehicles can be found at the corner of this road and a hunting camp driveway. To reach this crossing, follow Benner Run Road north from the beach at Black Moshannon State Park. After 1.9 miles, turn left onto Huckleberry Road, and follow this road uphill for 0.4 mile to the next junction. Turn right onto Meyers Run Road and travel another 0.7 mile to the hunting camp driveway that (at the time of writing) is marked by a sign bearing the address 1579. This access point is not recommended in winter.

To reach the AFT from here, walk north on the road for a short distance around a curve, where you will see the trail crossing with a post sign. This is the 30.96 mi point on the trail. A little further north on the road, there are some wide areas where a few more vehicles can park, but those spots are only recommended for sturdier vehicles.

BENNER RUN ROAD (Moose Head Lane)

GPS LOCATION: N40° 56.042' W78° 01.422'

The northeastern portions of the AFT are quite remote and difficult to reach by road. Benner Run Road leads to a spur trail that can be used as intermediate access. This access trail makes use of a hunting camp driveway that the locals have nicknamed Moose Head Lane.

Take Benner Run Road north then east from the beach at Black Moshannon State Park and stay on the road for 4.3 miles. Shortly before your destination, Benner Run Road passes over a height of land and makes a U-turn in a hollow. Proceed to a low point where there is a post sign for Moose Head Lane, which is a one-lane driveway. This point is just before a stone hunting camp and an excellent piped spring on opposite sides of the road; this is also 2.1 miles from the eastern end of Benner Run Road at Rattlesnake Pike.

Parking for a couple of vehicles is available along the north side of the road. Note that this spot requires volunteers to keep it clear, so the grass may get high. While adventurous hunting camp residents drive down Moose Head Lane, this is not recommended for all but the sturdiest vehicles, and hikers should park on Benner Run Road.

Begin walking down Moose Head Lane (northbound) and descend past a hunting camp to an alarmingly rickety bridge over Benner Run. Here you can see that some hunting camp residents seem to be driving right around this bridge and through the creek, and with good reason. Continue past several more hunting camps.

At the final camp, walk up the right side of the cul-de-sac at the end of the road, then turn right on an unblazed but fairly obvious grassy lane. Continue downhill as the grassy lane fades out and becomes a footpath marked occasionally with light blue blazes. Hop over a small run and reach the Allegheny Front Trail at an unsigned junction at its 33.67 mi point. The total length of Moose Head Lane/Trail is 0.67 mi (1.09 km). The approach on Benner Run Road can be hazardous in the winter.

Other AFT Road Crossings: The AFT also crosses Clay Mine Road and Six Mile Run Road in the southwestern portion of the trail, and Tram Road in the northeastern portion. However, due to a lack of nearby parking at the first two, and rough driving conditions on the latter, none of these are recommended as access for most hikers.

AFFILIATED TRAILS

NORTH END OF MOSS HANNE TRAIL
GPS LOCATION: N40° 54.060' W78° 03.674'

The Moss-Hanne Trail is reached via West Side Road, which begins just to the west of the PA 504 bridge over the lake at the center of Black Moshannon State Park. Follow this paved road south for 1.3 miles, along the edge of the lake and past various tourist cabins and boat launching areas. The road ends at a cul-de-sac with a small parking area that offers access to the MHT and a few other nearby nature trails.

SOUTH END OF SHINGLE MILL TRAIL
GPS LOCATION: N40° 55.110' W78° 03.581'

The Shingle Mill Trail is reached via Benner Run Road, which begins at the parking area for the beach at the center of Black Moshannon State Park. Drive north on Benner Run Road for 0.2 mile. Shortly after the end of the pavement, find a small parking area on the left that serves a picnic area as well as the SMT.

ROCK RUN TRAIL SYSTEM/AFT PARKING LOT
GPS LOCATION: N40° 55.016' W77° 58.617'

This is the same lot described above as the trailhead for the AFT, at the corner of PA 504 and Tram Road, 4.5 miles east of the intersection with Beaver Road in the center of Black Moshannon State Park.

GUIDE TO THE ALLEGHENY FRONT TRAIL

This description begins at the trailhead parking lot that is shared by the Allegheny Front Trail and the Rock Run Trails System. The description begins in the southbound (clockwise) direction from this starting point (see the *Access and Logistics* chapter above for more details).

SECTION 1: SOUTHEAST—
RATTLESNAKE PIKE (EAST CROSSING) TO BLACK MOSHANNON STATE PARK

MI	KM	DESCRIPTION
0.00	0.00	From the Allegheny Front Trail/Rock Run Trails System parking lot, cross Rattlesnake Pike (PA 504) and begin the Allegheny Front Trail in a southerly direction. Use caution while crossing the road, because even though Rattlesnake Pike does not see much traffic, the speed limit is 55 MPH. Here the trail is marked by yellow rectangular blazes. (Note: if you choose to go north from here, you will be following both the yellow blazes of the AFT and the blue blazes of the RRTS.)
0.13	0.21	Cross a barely visible grassy lane, which is known on some maps as Stagecoach Trail or Stagecoach Road, though "Stagecoach" is probably an historical inaccuracy. [Seeley, 81]

MI	KM	DESCRIPTION
0.15	0.24	Bear left onto an old road grade and begin a steep and rocky descent. This track is often erroneously referred to as an old stagecoach road. Evidence indicates that it is descended from a branch of the Great Shamokin Path used by Native Americans. In any case, any vehicle that traveled this road up and down the Allegheny Front was in for a terrifying journey. [Seeley, 81]
0.36	0.58	At a post sign, turn right abruptly off the road, climb a rocky embankment, then bear left. Watch the blazes carefully before and after this turn. Begin a steep but brief climb up a rocky slope. You can see the Allegheny Front dropping away to the left, down toward Bald Eagle Valley.
0.51	0.82	The trail levels off and you pass a former vista on the left, which has become overgrown. There is a nice view when the leaves are down.
0.58	0.93	Turn right onto an overgrown old logging road.
0.61	0.99	Watch very carefully for an abrupt left turn, off the old track and onto a footpath. You have missed this turn if you amble into a recent logging zone.
0.90	1.44	Reach the first major vista on the Allegheny Front Trail. The view is to the southeast, down a hollow that snakes between some foothills at the bottom of the Front, followed by the narrow and hidden Bald Eagle Valley, then Bald Eagle Ridge, then the equally hidden Nittany Valley, and finally Tussey Mountain across the back of the view. Several villages and one significant metro area (State College) are hidden within the folds of the rugged landscape. The AFT turns sharply left at this vista and descends into Whetstone Hollow.
0.95	1.53	Turn sharply right along a dry streambed in Whetstone Hollow. A stream may be flowing weakly during wet periods. Begin a steep descent featuring very unstable, rocky footway.

The first of many vistas to be seen from the Allegheny Front Trail.

MI	KM	DESCRIPTION
1.28	2.06	The trail begins a moderately strenuous climb back to the crest of the Allegheny Front. The terrain is still very rocky.
1.45	2.34	Turn sharply right and begin a steep climb alongside another rocky streambed. During wet periods you may hear a hidden stream under the boulder field to the left.
1.50	2.41	Turn left and cross the streambed next to a spring. This is followed by two more intermittent springs, after which the trail continues up the opposite side of the hollow. Water quality at the springs is acceptable, but there is usually very little of it, especially in the fall and winter.
1.67	2.68	Turn sharply right, then left, up a switchback that returns you to the crest of the Front.

MI	KM	DESCRIPTION
1.77	2.85	Reach another vista to the left, just after crossing a fern-filled area. At the time of writing, this vista needs to be cleared out due to growing trees, and the view is narrow. The trail then levels off and continues rather easily for a while, and when the leaves are down there are nearly continuous views to the left. There are also a few comfortable but dry campsites in this area.
1.94	3.13	Turn left and descend into a minor side hollow.
2.07	3.33	The trail bears right and begins to climb out of the side hollow.
2.21	3.55	Turn sharply right at a rugged rock outcropping and climb steeply back to the crest of the Front.
2.29	3.68	Another vista down into Bald Eagle Valley, at another good dry campsite.
2.40	3.86	Turn left and descend briefly into a gulch with some large boulders, then climb back out.

Ralph's Pretty Good View, a short distance from the AFT via a side trail.

MI	KM	DESCRIPTION
2.56	4.12	Reach the crest of the Front again, in an area with a few narrow vistas when the leaves are up, and nearly continuous views when the leaves are down.
3.02	4.87	Watch for a side trail on the left, which leads a short distance to the modestly named Ralph's Pretty Good View. This might be the best vista on the AFT, with more than 180 degrees of visibility if you scramble down the slope a bit. Beaver Road can be seen weaving through the foothills below. On a clear day, to the left (northeast) you can see what appears to be the end of Bald Eagle Ridge, but this is actually where the ridge curves away from your line of sight, about 40 miles from here in the Lock Haven area. Straight ahead (southeast), behind Bald Eagle Ridge you can see various sections of the State College metro area, with Nittany Mountain erupting from the valley floor and marching off to the northeast. Behind State College, Tussey Mountain is a straight line across most of your field of vision, reaching for dozens of miles to the right, while stopping abruptly and being replaced by other ridges behind Nittany Mountain to the left.
3.23	5.21	Reach Ralph's Majestic Vista. The two Ralph vistas are named after Ralph Seeley, the leading inspiration for the AFT. Much of the State College metro area is visible, as is Tussey Mountain Ski Area on a clear day. This is one of the premier vistas on a hiking trail in all of Pennsylvania. The view has been featured in many photographs of classic Central Pennsylvania scenery. [Seeley, 79] With a little bushwhacking downhill, you may be able to see a wider view but in this case the news is not so good. To the right you might see an environmentally calamitous gash in Bald Eagle Ridge, blasted out for Interstate 99 in the early 2000s.
3.28	5.28	The AFT bears right, away from the Allegheny Front and its vistas for good. Begin a moderate climb over some remaining sub-ridges at the very top.

MI	KM	DESCRIPTION
3.32	5.35	Climb through an interesting rock outcropping with very large boulders. Some hand-over-foot scrambling may be necessary. Afterwards, begin a gentle descent away from the Front. The AFT suddenly becomes much less rocky than before and is quite easy for about the next half mile.
3.81	6.13	Cross Underwood Road and continue straight ahead, through an open area where a few vehicles can park. After this crossing, the blazes change to yellow/red to denote a multi-use segment. Next, bear left at the back of the grassy area then continue on a gentle old lane that is likely an old camp driveway. [Seeley, 78–79]
4.01	6.45	Turn left onto trail. The AFT becomes moderately rocky again and begins a gentle climb to the top of the plateau. Starting around 2014, there has been extensive logging in this area.
4.41	7.10	The trail curves broadly to the right at the foot of a minor ridgeline.
4.46	7.18	The trail levels off at the height of land. The hiking is uneventful for about the next six-tenths of a mile.
5.08	8.18	The AFT is now descending on what appears to be an old logging road.
5.11	8.22	Bear right onto what is clearly an old logging road. About 90 yards later, bear right again onto yet another old logging road.
5.33	8.58	Where the logging road fizzles out, bear right onto trail.
5.53	8.90	Cross a one-lane dirt road that is called the Smays Trail on state forest maps. To the left, this trail/road leads uphill 0.82 mi (1.32 km) to the corner of Underwood Road and Beaver Road, where parking is available. After crossing the road, continue straight ahead toward a former car campsite.
5.56	8.95	Bear left at the back edge of the campsite, enter the trees, and then immediately turn right at a trail junction.

MI	KM	DESCRIPTION
5.61	9.03	Turn left into a grove of hemlock and red pine along Smays Run. This is the best campsite on the southeastern section of the AFT, and Smays Run is the best water source in the area as well. Next, cross a footbridge over the run and continue into a pleasant meadow. After the meadow, the trail is uneventful for about the next seven-tenths of a mile, first rising gently and then descending gently.
6.30	10.15	Reach an unnecessarily confusing trail junction at a post sign, where you will bear right. Here the AFT and the other trail are both blazed yellow/red. To the left is the access trail that comes in from the parking area at the corner of Beaver Road and Strawband Beaver Road. That trail is 0.19 mi (0.31 km) long. Adding to the confusion, the sign has an error as of the time of writing. The trail to the right (west) is not the Moss-Hanne Trail. Instead, the trail leading to the west is your next segment of the AFT, which leads to the beginning of the Moss-Hanne Trail a short distance from here.
6.48	10.44	Cross Beaver Road and enter Black Moshannon State Park. Use caution because of the limited visibility for drivers. Parking at this crossing is not recommended; the parking area at the corner of Strawband Beaver Road is just beyond the curve to the left and is reached via the short access trail described in the last entry. Next, the AFT continues in a westerly direction toward Black Moshannon Lake, and the blazes switch to yellow-only. For the next 3.44 mi (5.53 km) the AFT is within the boundaries of the state park, and no primitive camping is permitted. This spot is also the beginning of the Moss-Hanne Trail (MHT), which traverses a large portion of the state park and goes around the southern half of the lake. In the late 1990s the AFT was added to a portion of the previously existing MHT, so you will follow both for the next 2.78 mi (4.48 km). The MHT is also described in its own chapter later in this book.

The boardwalk through the Black Moshannon wetlands.

MI	KM	DESCRIPTION
6.51	10.48	The beginning of a system of boardwalks that carry the trail over wetlands that drain into the southern end of Black Moshannon Lake. The boardwalks can be slippery when wet but are a treat for hikers of all levels of ability.
6.54	10.53	The boardwalk rises and forms a bridge over Shirks Run, an unusually deep and fast-flowing stream. Note the coloration of the water, which some locals have compared to Dr. Pepper. The coloration is caused by decaying plant matter from the unique flora of the region, though the water remains mostly clear. This phenomenon provides the Black Moshannon area with its name. Downstream from the lake, Black Moshannon Creek retains its distinctive coloration for the rest of its distance.
6.60	10.63	First break in the boardwalk. Note the patches of soft and springy sphagnum moss along the trail. Watch your footing carefully along the non-boardwalk segments, which are often muddy. After this there are several more breaks in the boardwalk, taking advantage of occasional dry areas in this extensive wetland complex. [Seeley, 96]

MI	KM	DESCRIPTION
6.67	10.74	End of the boardwalk, followed immediately by an especially waterlogged section of old puncheon, and finally dry forest. Note the unique trees and shrubs in this area.
6.70	10.79	Enter a red pine plantation. Note the regular placement and uniform size of most of the trees, plus the general absence of other tree species in the area. The Black Moshannon region was extensively planted with red pine during the development of the state park, and you will see many such projects along the AFT. The trail is easy and uneventful for about the next half mile.
7.16	11.53	Cross a stream on logs.
7.24	11.66	Mile 7 marker, facing in the opposite direction. This distance applies to the Moss-Hanne Trail and is not relevant for the AFT. The trail is regularly muddy for about a mile in this area, because you are traversing the edge of a wetland.
7.94	12.79	The southern end of Black Moshannon Lake, and its bordering swamps and bogs, can be seen through the trees straight ahead. This area regularly features beaver dams.
8.01	12.90	Cross a small meadow filled with unique water-loving grasses and shrubs. The lake is visible to the right.
8.12	13.08	Begin a series of narrow plank boardwalks, built by Keystone Trails Association in 2018 in an attempt to rise above the mud.
8.23	13.26	Mile 6 marker for the MHT.
8.43	13.58	Enter another large meadow. This one has a variety of both dry and wet plant species.
8.49	13.68	As of 2024, there is an enormous beaver pond just to the right of the trail, formed by an impressive dam that is at least 200 feet long. The pond nearly reaches the trail.

MI	KM	DESCRIPTION
8.60	13.84	Footbridge over a stream. Next, enter another large soggy meadow, with an extensive wetland visible to the right. Patches of sand appear underfoot.
8.70	14.01	Enter the first of five small red pine plantations, which are separated by brief interludes of meadow or unplanned forest.
9.01	14.52	Cross a small stream on a footbridge. Water quality is acceptable except during dry periods.
9.18	14.78	At a post sign, turn right onto a woods road. (To the left, this lane leads 0.15 mi [0.24 km] to the small parking area at the corner of Shirks and Dug Roads.)
9.22	14.85	Mile 5 marker for the MHT.
9.26	14.92	Junction with the Moss-Hanne Trail at another post sign. From here, the AFT turns left and heads west toward Shirks Road. Beware that both trails are blazed yellow. The parking area nearest to this junction is at the corner of Shirks and Dug Roads, via the grassy lane that was described two entries above. (Straight ahead, the MHT continues northbound around the west side of Black Moshannon Lake. See the separate MHT trail description later in this book.)

SECTION 2: SOUTHWEST—
BLACK MOSHANNON STATE PARK TO RATTLESNAKE PIKE (WEST CROSSING)

MI	KM	DESCRIPTION
9.26	14.92	Turn left (west) at the junction with the Moss-Hanne Trail. Beware that both trails are blazed yellow.
9.67	15.57	A spring emerges from under trees to the left of the trail. Water quality is adequate once it starts flowing. Next, turn left and cross the stream formed by the spring.
9.92	15.97	Turn right on Shirks Road. This is also the outer boundary of Black Moshannon State Park, so primitive camping will be permitted after the AFT departs from Shirks Road. The AFT follows this road through a large open area with low-lying shrubbery and a few stunted trees. This area acts as a transitional wetland, supplied by the upper reaches of Black Moshannon Creek.
9.98	16.07	Road bridge over Black Moshannon Creek. Here the creek has not yet obtained its distinctive dark coloration. Water quality is questionable.
10.00	16.10	On the left, note the historical sign describing Bald Eagle's Path, which originated in ancestral times as a Native American footpath that led from the present Bald Eagle Valley east of here all the way to Presque Isle at the present city of Erie in northwestern Pennsylvania. The path was later expanded into a stagecoach road for settlers, which was then replaced by a turnpike and finally by the modern PA 504. Meanwhile, there is a grassy area on the left that can handle one or two cars. To the right is Lucky Ridge Camp, which has an excellent spring along the right edge of the yard. Do not park in the camp's driveway.

Historical sign describing Bald Eagle's Path

MI	KM	DESCRIPTION
10.05	16.19	Turn left off of Shirks Road. The trail remains roughly parallel to the road for a while. Until the late 2010s, the AFT turned off of Shirks Road back at the sign for Bald Eagle's Path, and then went south alongside the Black Moshannon wetlands through an area that was prone to blowdowns and mud pits. You have just turned onto a new relocation that is just to the west of the old version of the trail but goes through a noticeably different landscape.
10.11	16.28	Curve broadly to the left (south).
10.17	16.38	Trail register; please sign in.
10.24	16.48	Pass a deep hole on the right and the end of a soggy artificial trench on the left. This is probably the site of an old homestead or business that brought water down a canal for some mechanical purpose such as turning a water wheel. Next, enter a young forest that has grown since a logging operation around the turn of the millennium.

MI	KM	DESCRIPTION
10.46	16.84	Short plank boardwalk over a muddy area.
10.99	17.70	Turn right at an old trail junction. Next there are some more short plank boardwalks.
11.09	17.87	After a brief dry area, continue on some more plank boardwalks. The upper reaches of the Black Moshannon wetlands can be seen through the trees to the left.
11.22	18.07	Enter a shady grove of hemlocks and white pines, which indicate that there is reliable water nearby.
11.34	18.26	Turn abruptly right in a great camping spot; watch the blazes carefully. Shortly after the turn, you reach Black Moshannon Creek: acceptable water quality. Here the creek is a modest babbling brook not too far from its source. This same creek feeds the large wetland complex that you traversed a few miles ago and was dammed to form the enormous lake at the state park. Downstream from the dam, the much deeper and wider Black Moshannon Creek accompanies most of the Shingle Mill Trail, and the AFT will encounter it again about 20 hiker miles ahead.
11.37	18.30	Curve away from the creek and walk along the left edge of a meadow. The trail soon re-enters the trees and reunites with the creek, with more camping spots on both sides.
11.50	18.51	Pass a couple of small waterfalls in the stream. At the time of writing, someone had contributed an old office chair to the campsite on the other side.
11.69	18.82	Curve right and begin rising away from the Black Moshannon watershed. The elevation gain is modest; but note the change in plant life as you enter a higher-altitude forest.
11.81	19.01	Cross a heavily overgrown old logging road, with scrubby meadows visible to the right.

Upper Black Moshannon Creek as a babbling brook, long before it feeds a massive lake and wetland complex.

MI	KM	DESCRIPTION
11.83	19.05	Cross Clay Mine Road. At the time of writing, no parking was available within sight of this crossing. The AFT blazes switch to yellow/red to mark a multi-use segment.
12.14	19.55	A small open meadow can be seen to the right of the trail. Note the differences between the plant life in this dry meadow and that in the wet meadows of Black Moshannon.
12.47	20.07	Reach a height of land, after a long gentle climb.
12.80	20.61	Turn left onto a logging road.
12.83	20.65	Bear left at a junction of woods roads.
13.12	21.14	Before reaching the vehicle gate that is visible ahead, turn right abruptly onto trail. There is a post sign here; but watch the blazes carefully nonetheless.

MI	KM	DESCRIPTION
13.15	21.18	Turn right onto an active pipeline swath. The blazes have changed back to yellow-only.
13.18	21.22	Continue straight ahead, past a valve apparatus and a junction with another pipeline swath.
13.58	21.87	Still on the pipeline, cross an upper tributary of Six Mile Run on a snowmobile bridge. Note the ruins of a previous bridge below. The stream is usually hidden under dense vegetation and is not a handy source of drinking water.
13.63	21.95	Turn right onto trail, shortly before the pipeline swath begins to climb. Watch blazes carefully.
13.84	22.28	Bear right then left through a small hemlock grove, but do not cross the stream. Watch blazes carefully.
13.87	22.34	Great campsite in another hemlock grove. The water in the passing stream is of questionable quality, but there is an outstanding spring a little further down the trail. [Seeley, 94]
13.89	22.37	Cross a log next to the spring (excellent water quality). Watch your footing carefully on the next section of trail, which is on narrow sidehill above a wet area.
13.99	22.53	The trail joins what appears to be an old narrow-gauge railroad grade.
14.04	22.61	Enter another good campsite along the stream. Water quality is questionable but may have improved since the last campsite.
14.07	22.65	Turn left, then right, climbing away from the stream. The trail then levels off on a sub-ridge above the stream.
14.27	22.98	Cross a grassy lane and begin a steep climb.
14.54	23.42	Turn right in a dark hemlock grove and descend.

MI	KM	DESCRIPTION
14.56	23.45	After a broad curve to the left to parallel Six Mile Run Road, the AFT enters Wolf Rocks. This extensive outcropping of large boulders is both scenic and utilitarian, which the hiker will notice upon seeing vast amounts of porcupine and deer droppings in the sheltered, overhanging areas. There are legends of buried treasure at Wolf Rocks. [Seeley, 94] Watch your footing very carefully through the Wolf Rocks area.
14.67	23.63	Cross Six Mile Run Road. This point is the AFT's closest approach to US 322, which is less than two miles to the southwest via Horse Hollow Road. However, there is no convenient parking within sight of this crossing.
14.71	23.68	Cross Six Mile Run on a footbridge. Before the mid-2010s, the trail crossed an old stone dam here and the area to the left was filled with a clogged-up artificial lake, which in turn had been utilized by an old sawmill a century before. [Seeley, 94] The dam and lake were removed, and Six Mile Run was restored to its natural course.
14.77	23.78	Emerge at a complex intersection of trail, dirt road, and old railroad grade. Bear right on the grassy railroad grade that leads around the back of a hunting camp. Do not turn sharply right onto the driveway that leads to the front of the camp.
14.90	24.00	Bear right briefly on an artificial embankment before hopping down the other side. This is the remains of a very long earthen dam that once created a large artificial lake, which was utilized by a substantial logging and milling operation on Six Mile Run in the early 1900s. As a brief side-trip, some history can be observed if you follow the embankment toward the creek. In 1976 a second, smaller dam was built at this location by Ducks Unlimited to create a fishing spot. [Seeley, 94] By the new millennium that dam had become leaky, and its pond was mostly filled with silt. In 2010, Clearwater Conservancy of State College spearheaded a project to dismantle the Ducks Unlimited dam, drain the pond, restore Six Mile

MI	KM	DESCRIPTION
(cont.)		Run to its original course, and replant the area with native vegetation. This location has illustrated the ultimate fate of all dams, not just once but twice!
15.20	24.48	Nice campsite amidst hemlocks next to Six Mile Run. Water from Six Mile Run should be treated before drinking because the creek has collected many tributaries of undependable quality.
15.25	24.55	Turn left away from the creek and climb up the side of the hollow.
15.29	24.62	The AFT curves broadly to the left and enters Slide Hollow. This is a significant side hollow of Six Mile Run, but surprisingly it contains only an intermittent stream that is almost always dry. The hollow was indeed used as a giant slide during the logging era. [Seeley, 93]
15.37	24.76	The trail bears right and begins a gradual descent toward the bottom of Slide Hollow.
15.56	25.06	Walk through a low point in Slide Hollow. The trail then curves widely to the left and begins a mildly strenuous ascent up the hollow. The climb is long but uneventful.
16.37	26.36	After a long and steady climb, the trail is now on relatively high ground between multiple dry streambeds.
16.43	26.46	Turn right and scramble briefly to the height of land near the very top of Slide Hollow. The AFT levels off, and the hiking is easy and rather uneventful for about the next two miles. The forest is thin is this area for multiple reasons: it is on a windy plateau-top, there are regular logging operations, and the forest is still recovering from a decades-past gypsy moth infestation. [Seeley, 93]
17.61	28.36	Cross two parallel trenches of mysterious origin. These may be eroded drainage channels that formed along both edges of an artificially raised railroad grade.

MI	KM	DESCRIPTION
17.71	28.52	Turn right and descend into a shallow saucer-shaped depression on top of the plateau. Ahead, note how rocks have accumulated at the low point in this dip in the landscape, which likely took thousands of years.
17.89	28.81	Begin climbing back out to the top of the plateau. To the right, you can see the shallow depression being funneled into a side hollow that leads down to Six Mile Run.
18.11	29.16	After leveling off briefly, the trail descends into another shallow depression in the otherwise flat plateau landscape. This one also feeds a descending hollow to the right. The white-blazed state forest boundary can be seen paralleling the trail to the left.
18.32	29.50	The AFT curves right and descends steeply into Six Mile Run canyon.
18.47	29.74	Emerge at the corner of Six Mile Run Road and Clay Mine Road. The AFT continues straight ahead, following Clay Mine Road downhill. Just before the road bridge, parking is available on the right. Do not park on the left in front of the hunting camp.
18.53	29.85	Cross the road bridge over Six Mile Run. Next, bear left at the road junction onto Shields Dam Road.
18.56	29.89	Almost immediately after the fork in the road, turn left abruptly onto trail. Watch carefully for a post sign at this turn.
18.59	29.93	After crossing a small run, turn left onto a well-defined logging road. This road ascends gently through an extensive evergreen plantation, containing thousands of trees (mostly red pine) and covering dozens of acres. The evergreens were planted by the Civilian Conservation Corps and the PA Bureau of Forestry starting in the 1930s. The workers are to be commended for their efforts in reforesting Central Pennsylvania after the logging era, though some outdoor lovers may feel

MI	KM	DESCRIPTION
(cont.)		disconcerted by the unnatural order and sameness of this planted forest. The monotonous plantation to the right of the trail contrasts sharply with the more varied, and less managed, forest to the left that leads down to Six Mile Run. [Seeley, 92]
18.80	30.28	A log slide plunges down the hillside from the right, while the white-blazed State Forest boundary appears on the left. The logging road, still paralleling Six Mile Run, levels off but becomes overgrown.
19.19	30.90	Scramble into and out of a heavily entrenched dry run. The unusual depth of this modest watercourse is probably due to intensified soil erosion when the hillside was denuded of trees during the logging era. The trail then starts to climb.
19.36	31.18	Cross a shrub-filled open area that extends downhill— possibly an abandoned pipeline swath. This is one of the outer edges of the huge red pine plantation, followed by a bit of more wild forest.
19.38	31.20	Turn right in a hemlock grove, quickly pass back into the red pine plantation, and begin a vigorous climb.
19.53	31.45	The trail levels off at the top of the canyon and passes through a few patches of more varied forest.
19.65	31.64	Enter an upper corner of the red pine plantation. This parcel on top of the hill looks a little less intensively managed than the parts of the plantation back in the hollow, and some other tree species have managed to establish themselves.
19.81	31.90	The trail curves to the left and enters a much more varied forest. There are still many red pines along the trail, but they are of variable age and appear not to have been planted in a pattern. This indicates that these trees are probably colonists from the plantation, grown from cones that were transported by animals or the elements.

MI	KM	DESCRIPTION
20.00	32.20	Cross an old logging road.
20.41	32.87	Cross a pipeline swath with access road, then begin descending into a scenic side hollow of Six Mile Run.
20.65	33.25	Enter a pleasant little canyon with many and varied evergreens. This is a good area for nature photography. The trail follows an old railroad grade built slightly up the right side of the hollow.
20.77	33.44	The trail begins to slab higher up the side of the hollow, staying relatively level, while a rapidly descending stream appears in the bottom of the canyon to the left.
20.87	33.60	The trail curves to the right along a bench in the side of the mountain. Six Mile Run, which is now a sizeable creek, can be heard and occasionally seen far down the canyon to the left.
20.98	33.79	Turn left and begin a steep, rocky descent toward the creek.
21.02	33.85	Reach the bank of Six Mile Run, and bear right downstream. There are many tempting campsites along Six Mile Run, in this area and also later on the other side of PA 504. However, not all of the campsites are a sufficient distance from the water, per state forest regulations. As described earlier, water from the creek should be treated, and do not drink water from overflow channels or backwaters.
21.17	34.09	After a short stretch inland, briefly reunite with Six Mile Run and then bear right and climb away from the bank. Watch the blazes carefully. The climb is steep and rocky, but brief, and tops out on a short section of old railroad grade.
21.24	34.20	Rejoin Six Mile Run. More campsites have been established along the banks, though once again not all the spots are an acceptable distance from the creekside.

MI	KM	DESCRIPTION
21.29	34.29	Turn right, away from the creek once again, and begin another steep but brief climb. The trail soon joins an old logging railroad grade and levels off, following a bench built into the hillside. Curiously, this is not the same railroad grade that appeared above the last climb away from Six Mile Run, just a couple of hundred yards back as the crow flies. [Seeley, 91–92]
21.38	34.42	The railroad grade curves to the right and enters Hutton Hollow. You can now hear traffic on PA 504. Enter an area of impressive giant rhododendron bushes.
21.60	34.78	Watch the blazes very carefully for a sharp left turn, off the railroad grade and onto what appears to be an old log slide toward Hutton Run. Here, logs may have been removed from train cars on the railroad and slid down to the run for further floating downstream. [Seeley, 91] (If you miss this turn, the railroad grade continues straight ahead as a blue-blazed but rather overgrown spur trail. The spur leads east approximately 1.5 miles to Airport Road near Mid State Airport.)
21.64	34.84	After a steep descent, bear left along Hutton Run. This is a pretty nice little hollow, if you ignore the presence of high-speed Rattlesnake Pike (PA 504) just on the other side of the stream.
21.72	34.97	Turn right on a hunting camp driveway and cross the bridge over Hutton Run.
21.74	35.00	Cross Rattlesnake Pike. This is a potentially dangerous crossing, as the speed limit is 45 MPH along hills and sharp curves in both directions. The visibility for drivers is especially restricted. To the left, on the other side of Six Mile Run, there is a staggered intersection with Six Mile Run Road. Plentiful parking is available at both corners.

SECTION 3: NORTHWEST—
RATTLESNAKE PIKE (WEST CROSSING) TO SHINGLE MILL TRAIL

MI	KM	DESCRIPTION
21.74	35.00	The AFT hops over the guard rail on the north side of Rattlesnake Pike and continues parallel to Six Mile Run downstream (northbound).
21.80	35.10	Descend on nice stone steps to Six Mile Run. There is an island in the creek to the left.
21.90	35.26	Veer inland into a nice grove of hemlock and giant rhododendron.
22.01	35.44	The trail slabs up the side of the hollow, on nice sidehill construction, then descends back to the creek.
22.27	35.87	Enter a bucolic little grove with mossy rocks and giant rhododendron. Watch blazes carefully. The trail begins to rise above the creek again.
22.37	36.02	Switchback down to the creek once more, with some stone steps. Enter a zone of bottomland forest, with some different tree species than in the evergreen-heavy forest inhabiting the sides of the hollow.
22.62	36.43	Cross the outlet of an outstanding spring, which is actually an underground run blasting out from under a tree to the right of the trail. Excellent water quality, except during dry periods.
22.80	36.72	The trail squeezes between the creekside and an impressive overhang of boulders. After a heavy rain, the rocks drip with water released from the tree roots above. The remains of a stone dam, associated with the large Plumbe Forge operation nearby, can be seen in the creekbed. [Seeley, 89–90] There are a few more rock outcroppings ahead.

MI	KM	DESCRIPTION
22.90	36.87	Another large spring appears next to the trail (questionable water quality). Cross the outflow stream on rocks. Next is a small campsite under hemlocks. Beyond the campsite, seeps and springs appear along the trail regularly, creating a general wet area. Watch footing carefully.
23.12	37.22	The trail slabs steeply up the hillside, around a small landslide, then descends gently back to the creek on what appears to be an old railroad grade.
23.22	37.39	Bear left across an intersection with an old woods road, cross a low area on rocks, and head toward a grove of red and white pines. Excellent campsite.
23.35	37.60	The remains of another old stone dam are visible in the creek. For a while beyond this point, the trail tries to stay alongside Six Mile Run, but has to briefly ascend and descend several times, around rocky areas or dense rhododendron thickets.
23.82	38.35	Emerge at a side channel of the main creek, with a fairly large island to the left. Next, pass through some especially dense rhododendron and reach Six Mile Run again.
23.99	38.62	Nice campsite, through which flow two streams formed by large springs. Water quality is questionable. Next are another quick ascent and descent with stone steps and expert sidehill construction.
24.11	38.82	Reach Six Mile Run once again, at another acceptable campsite.
24.20	38.98	Enter an excessively dense thicket of rhododendron, which forces several curves into the trail. This area is prone to excessive overgrowth; if the path is clear at the time of your hike, give thanks to trail care volunteers and state forest personnel.
24.40	39.29	In a small wet meadow, turn right, cross an overflow channel, and quickly switchback up an embankment.

MI	KM	DESCRIPTION
24.45	39.37	Mysterious remains of a small stone building, possibly a stable for draft animals used during the logging era. This hut is now swamped by small trees and giant rhododendron bushes. [Seeley, 89]
24.59	39.59	Turn right, cross a side stream, and begin climbing away from Six Mile Run.
24.65	39.69	After a steep and very rocky climb, turn left. The trail levels off briefly but soon begins climbing again, sometimes on stone steps. The AFT is now tackling a minor ridgeline that juts into a corner of land between Six Mile Run and Moshannon Creek.
24.72	39.80	Reach the top of the ridgeline, then begin an equally steep and rocky descent through dense rhododendron. Watch blazes carefully on the way down.
24.83	39.98	Turn right, uphill, on Casanova Road (which is known as Munson Road on some maps). This road carries some moderate traffic, and the sight distance for drivers is very limited, so exercise caution while walking up the road.
24.88	40.06	Turn left off the road and scramble down a steep embankment that may be an old log slide. [Seeley, 88] The trail quickly levels off on a well-defined old railroad grade through varied forest. Red Moshannon Creek becomes visible for the first time down to the left. See the sidebar below.

SIDEBAR: MOSHANNON CREEK

Moshannon Creek, one of the principal waterways of the plateau region of Centre and Clearfield Counties, is known colloquially as the Red Moshannon or Red Mo due to its distinctive orange coloration. When viewed from the air, this bright orange ribbon of water is an especially outlandish sight.

The orange (dis-)coloration is the result of acid seepage from myriad old coal mines near the river's source, some dating as far back as the early

1800s. Even though most of the mines in question have been inactive for many decades, acid runoff continues to contaminate the groundwater and tributaries that feed the river. [Seeley, 77] This severe pollution has thus far resisted many governmental and nonprofit attempts at amelioration.

As it churns toward the West Branch of the Susquehanna River, Moshannon Creek cuts an impressive gorge into the Allegheny Plateau, resulting in some great vistas for hikers, as well as pleasant and scenic riverside rambling.

Each spring, snowmelt transforms the river into a noteworthy whitewater playground for rafting, canoeing, and kayaking. The annual Red Mo Downriver Race, which takes place a short distance downstream from the area traversed by the AFT, attracts paddling enthusiasts from across the northeastern United States.

Moshannon Creek is an outstanding recreational resource. Unfortunately, the river is devoid of aquatic life, and all the rocks in and around the streambed are stained with unsightly orange residue. This is a sad display of how pollution can persist for decades, and even centuries, after industrial ventures cease their short-lived operations.

BACK ON THE AFT

MI	KM	DESCRIPTION
24.96	40.20	Scramble up and around what appears to be an old landslide, which took the railroad grade with it. Rejoin the grade on the other side. The trail becomes a little more rugged and rocky.
25.10	40.41	Cross a small stream that plunges dramatically down the mountainside. Water quality is excellent, though exercise caution during dry periods. Interestingly, this stream disappears underground just to the left of the trail.
25.20	40.58	Jump over another plunging stream with excellent water quality (except, once again, during dry periods). The railroad grade underfoot has fizzled out, probably due to natural erosion processes on the mountainside. Continue ahead on trail.

MI	KM	DESCRIPTION
25.38	40.87	Cross yet another excellent high-quality (except during dry periods) stream plunging down the side of the canyon.
25.51	41.08	Turn right at the bottom of a jagged little side hollow. Begin climbing up the usually dry streambed. Oddly, this well-defined hollow does not carry a regular watercourse, while the above-noted streams plunge freestyle down the mountainside.
25.60	41.23	The trail bears left and slabs up the side of the hollow above the dry run. The climb becomes steep and rocky. This is the beginning of a strenuous ascent, leading part of the way to the top of the mountain above Moshannon Creek. Pass several large boulders on the way up.
25.76	41.48	Turn left at the top of the climb and begin descending.
25.86	41.65	A short side trail departs to the left and leads to a nice vista looking down over Moshannon Creek in the upstream direction. Back on the AFT, the descent becomes steep and rocky, leading into Sawdust Hollow.
26.07	41.99	Enter a generally flat area within Sawdust Hollow.
26.17	42.14	Cross Sawdust Run next to a scenic double waterfall. Water quality is excellent. Moshannon Creek is now a short distance to the left of the trail.
26.33	42.41	Hop over a spring (water quality questionable) that comes down the embankment from the right. The AFT now begins its closest approach to Moshannon Creek, along an old railroad grade beneath a variety of bottomland tree species. The railroad grade is in rough shape, probably from getting washed out regularly by floodwaters, and soon disappears altogether. Note: Now that you are alongside the Red Mo, it is unnecessary to risk drinking the acidic orange water, because the canyon has many springs and incoming streams with acceptable or better water quality, during all but the driest periods. Ralph Seeley reports that the

MI	KM	DESCRIPTION
(cont.)		Red Mo water has a tart lemonade-like taste due to its acid content; the water is not immediately hazardous to one's health; but imbibe at your own risk. [Seeley, 85]
26.39	42.49	Ascend and descend around a small hollowed-out area, with an excellent spring crossing the trail (during wet periods only). The trail continues on expert sidehill construction, frequently rising and falling while staying parallel to the river's edge.
26.48	42.65	Pass through a small open area with two spring outlets. Water quality in both is questionable. Out in the creek, wooden beams are visible under the water over by the opposite bank—the remains of a dam and milling operation. [Seeley, 87]
26.55	42.75	Enter a large, relatively open area that shows signs of past use, probably as a logging camp or river depot. The remains of a stone wall, possibly part of a pen for draft animals, can be seen to the right at the bottom of the hill. [Seeley, 86–87] Good camping in this area. Next, the trail bears left into a strip of land between the creek and a muddy backwater channel. Enter a section of floodplain forest featuring immense rhododendron bushes and tall, thin evergreens.
26.78	43.12	Turn right and cross the muddy backwater channel on logs. The trail then bears right and climbs up the embankment. Turn left at the top, then shortly thereafter turn right toward the roaring Tark Run.
26.86	43.25	Turn left to a wet crossing of Tark Run; good water quality. Next, the trail curves to the left back toward Moshannon Creek, but this time it does not return to the riverside.
26.99	43.47	The trail begins to slab up the hillside with very rocky footway, high above but still parallel to the river.
27.39	44.10	Enter an open rocky area, a bit removed from the creek. A lower floodplain is visible to the left.

MI	KM	DESCRIPTION
27.45	44.20	The trail joins a grassy lane—the remains of an old logging road.
27.52	44.31	Continue straight ahead at a woods road junction.
27.69	44.59	Keep left at a fork in the woods road. The AFT is still roughly parallel to Moshannon Creek, which remains visible through the trees to the left.
27.81	44.79	Cross the bottom of a shallow, dry side hollow. The woods road fades out underfoot. Watch the blazes carefully as the footway reverts to trail.
27.88	44.90	Cross Dry Run (questionable water quality). The name is a misnomer because this is a flowing stream for most of the year. Next, the trail returns to a densely wooded embankment above Moshannon Creek.
27.94	44.99	Cross the outlet of a strong spring that drops abruptly to the creek. Water quality is acceptable. Next, turn right, then left, while climbing up the rocky side of the canyon. This is yet another upward slab parallel to Moshannon Creek. The trail joins what appears to be an old narrow-gauge railroad grade.
28.03	45.14	Bear left at a junction with another railroad grade. Do not turn right; that grade carries a different blazed trail. (Be especially careful at this junction if you are going in the other direction.) The AFT levels off but remains quite rocky.
28.14	45.32	The AFT curves broadly right into Potter Hollow.
28.19	45.40	Turn sharply left toward a wet crossing of the rapidly plunging Potter Run. Water quality is acceptable. There are some possibilities for camping in this area.
28.32	45.60	The AFT is parallel to Moshannon Creek again and is following another old railroad grade. This one was sturdily built on a rock retaining wall, which was probably the result of lessons learned after many floods. Around this area you begin hearing traffic on I-80,

MI	KM	DESCRIPTION
(cont.)		sporadically at first but then continuously. The freeway's high viaduct over Moshannon Creek, downstream from here, can be seen occasionally through the trees ahead when the leaves are down.
28.82	46.42	Within sight of a truck-sized boulder in the river, begin a steep climb away from Moshannon Creek for good. This is the start of the most extensive climb on the AFT. Also, you have just walked through the lowest point on the AFT at about 1,320 feet in elevation, deep in the Red Mo canyon, so there is only one way to go from here.
28.90	46.54	Turn right at a switchback, then just 10 yards later, turn right again onto a heavily overgrown woods road, and continue climbing. Watch blazes carefully.
29.06	46.80	Continue straight ahead, still climbing, at a junction with another woods road. Your road grade is now better defined and easier to follow, though this area is low on blazes because of the lack of suitable trees. Meanwhile, noise from I-80 has become a constant din. The trail then levels off for a while through an open area that shows signs of past abuse and has been colonized by invasive plants.
29.20	47.01	Turn sharply left at another woods road junction. Watch for the road segment that rises rather than descends and continue climbing steeply. (If you are following the AFT in the other direction, be especially careful in this confusing, poorly blazed area.)
29.39	47.33	At the top of the climb, turn right at a four-way intersection of grassy lanes. There is a post sign at this junction. After the right turn at the sign, the AFT follows the next grassy lane uneventfully for about half a mile. The lane rises gently and first passes through a young high-altitude forest of thin, even-aged beech and birch trees. This is a recently clear-cut area, though the forest has managed to regenerate.

MI	KM	DESCRIPTION
(cont.)		(Back at the post sign, if you turn left, in a few minutes you can reach a vista back into Moshannon Creek canyon, in an area traversed by both the I-80 viaduct and an old railroad bridge. [Seeley, 85] Meanwhile, the lane straight ahead is an old logging road that proceeds parallel to the interstate.)
29.50	47.50	The woods road curves broadly to the left (southeast). The AFT continues a gentle ascent toward the top of the plateau. Potter Hollow becomes visible through the trees to the right. Traffic noise from I–80 can still be heard for a while, but eventually the silence of the forest prevails.
29.90	48.15	Enter an area where extensive logging and drilling commenced in the early 2010s. The formerly pleasant and easy grassy lane has been bulldozed into a hard gravel road that is exposed to the sun and continues to rise, creating an unpleasant slog for about the next nine-tenths of a mile. You will pass several intersections with other recently bulldozed roads of this type. In all cases, continue straight ahead.
30.74	49.50	A large hunting camp appears to the right. Continue straight ahead, still on the same logging road.
30.80	49.60	Turn left where the logging road meets the hunting camp's driveway. The AFT exits the active logging zone; but note the sparse nature of the forest even when it is not being logged. This area is still recovering from a forest fire set by an arsonist circa 1993. [Seeley, 85]
30.87	49.71	Turn left abruptly off the driveway and onto trail; watch the blazes carefully. The trail enters an open field with few trees and very dense ferns and huckleberry bushes. The footpath is rather hard to follow. (If you miss this turn, the driveway will soon bring you to Meyers Run Road, where you can turn left and proceed a short distance around a curve to the AFT crossing, which is marked by a post sign.)

MI	KM	DESCRIPTION
30.96	49.85	Cross Meyers Run Road. Parking for a few cars is available to the right, at the end of the driveway you were following a few minutes ago. Just after the road crossing, the AFT bears right along the edge of Black Moshannon hollow.
31.09	50.07	Turn sharply left and begin a steep descent. There are multiple switchbacks on the way down, so watch the blazes carefully. As you approach the bottom of the hollow, you will be able to hear the robust waters of Black Moshannon Creek, which at this point is downstream from the dam and lake in Black Moshannon State Park.
31.39	50.55	Reach the junction with the Shingle Mill Trail, where the AFT turns left. Beware that both trails have yellow blazes.

SECTION 4: NORTHEAST—
SHINGLE MILL TRAIL TO RATTLESNAKE PIKE (EAST CROSSING)

MI	KM	DESCRIPTION
31.39	50.55	Turn left at the junction with Shingle Mill Trail, which is also yellow-blazed. Meanwhile, please sign in at the trail register. The parking area nearest to this junction is back up at Meyers Run Road, 0.43 mi (0.70 km) west of here, as described three entries above. (To the right, the Shingle Mill Trail leads 3.67 mi [5.91 km] to Black Moshannon State Park. See the separate SMT trail description later in this book.)
31.70	51.05	Black Moshannon Creek comes into view for the first time, through a nice little grove of hemlocks to the right. This is a tempting campsite, though it's a little small and too close to the creek. Any water taken from Black Moshannon Creek should be treated prior to human consumption, because by this point it has collected many tributaries, and the water has passed through the lake and dam up at the state park.
31.85	51.28	Hop across a small side stream (water quality questionable), with an island in the Black Moshannon visible to the right. Next, the trail is on the bank of the creek for a while, sometimes right on the edge and sometimes rising and falling around rocky areas or copses of dense vegetation. The low points may be a bit treacherous during periods of high water.
31.96	51.47	The trail has veered inland a bit. Pass a nice campsite in a hemlock grove to the right, between the creek and a muddy backwater channel.
32.08	51.65	Turn left, cross a side stream of questionable quality, then turn right toward the creekside again.

MI	KM	DESCRIPTION
32.19	51.83	Emerge at a heavily used campsite and continue ahead. The confluence with Benner Run is visible on the opposite side of the creek. Note the dark but clear coloration of Black Moshannon Creek, due to decaying plant matter in the wetlands traversed by the AFT about 25 miles ago. Unlike the coalmine-based pollution on Red Moshannon Creek, the coloration process for the Black Moshannon is natural and is not harmful to the health of the creek.
32.21	51.86	Turn right and cross the long footbridge over Black Moshannon Creek. On the far side of the bridge, turn right at the front door of the hunting camp, head toward the incoming Benner Run, then turn left and head toward the high footbridge. Watch the blazes carefully.
32.25	51.93	Cross the well-built footbridge over the usually roaring and boisterous Benner Run, then turn left to follow the run upstream. Water quality in Benner Run is generally acceptable; but follow the general rule of not taking drinking water from sluggish or muddy side channels and backwaters.
32.36	52.11	Soon after reaching the bank of Benner Run again, hop across a tributary stream. There are many such springs and side streams as you head up Benner Run, with variable water quality.
32.47	52.28	Reach a nice resting spot, with a couple of large boulders over Benner Run.
32.54	52.39	Cross a small side channel. You'll soon see that this channel's water pops up from underground a few yards from the creekside. Benner Run features many such underground trickles of water, thanks to cracks and gaps in the underlying rock and spaces in the vast network of hemlock roots. You will cross this side channel a few more times ahead.

MI	KM	DESCRIPTION
32.92	53.02	First suitable campsite along Benner Run, in an open area between the trail and the creek.
33.00	53.14	Make a short ascent and descent on the embankment, around a small washed-out area. To the left, Benner Run has split into multiple braided channels of roughly equal flow, forming a couple of islands that are choked with impenetrable rhododendron.
33.22	53.49	Pass through a small open area. Just beyond, a short side trail to the left leads to a possible campsite that is adequately removed from the creekside, but very cramped.
33.29	53.61	Cross a little surprise meadow filled with huckleberry and other low-lying shrubbery, followed by an especially dense jungle of giant rhododendron.
33.39	53.76	Cross another well-built footbridge over Benner Run, continuing upstream.
33.52	53.97	Reach Mary's Window, where a little opening has been cut through the giant rhododendron to offer a picturesque view of a waterfall in Benner Run. Next, the AFT swings inland a bit, and mountain laurel abruptly replaces rhododendron as the dominant shrub. This indicates how much water each species prefers.
33.67	54.23	Turn left abruptly at an unsigned junction with a side trail. This is the Moose Head Lane Trail, which leads ahead to Benner Run Road in 0.67 mi (1.09 km). [Seeley, 83] After the turn, begin ascending into open high-altitude woods with heavy mountain laurel growth, alongside an intermittent run at first. The hillside becomes increasingly rocky on the way up.
33.86	54.53	Pass through an outcropping of large boulders. For about the next half mile, continue on a long drawn-out climb to the top of the plateau, though it is not particularly steep.

MI	KM	DESCRIPTION
34.46	55.49	The AFT has leveled off on top of the plateau, after making a broad curve to the left (north). The trail remains easy and uneventful for about the next half mile, through a thin forest.
35.06	56.46	Begin a mild descent into a shallow hollow.
35.33	56.89	Turn right abruptly; watch the blazes carefully. (If you miss this turn, a footpath continues ahead but soon becomes overgrown.) After the turn, the AFT begins a moderate climb to the top of a minor ridgeline.
35.44	57.07	Begin a steep but brief descent toward Hall Run.
35.51	57.18	Cross footbridge over Hall Run. Acceptable water quality in season.
35.68	57.46	Cross a usually dry streambed.
35.90	57.80	Cross another usually dry streambed. Note the soggy area to the right, which during wet periods becomes a small wetland that feeds the stream and sends water down to Hall Run.
35.95	57.89	Begin a mild climb. For about the next half mile, the AFT climbs gently to higher ground above the Hall Run watershed, and enters an area that has gone through a gypsy moth infestation and several rounds of salvage logging. [Seeley, 82]
36.46	58.71	The AFT curves broadly to the left and then begins descending gently into what appears to be a self-contained hollow. However, this is merely an upper bench of the unusually wide Rock Run valley.
36.61	58.95	Bear right and descend more steeply.
36.73	59.15	Cross Tram Road. After the road crossing, watch the blazes carefully through another recently logged area. To the right (south), Tram Road leads to PA 504 at the AFT/RRTS parking lot. Recent logging operations have resulted in some open spots that might provide parking near the trail crossing, though the drive to this point is rough.

MI	KM	DESCRIPTION
36.77	59.21	Enter a rocky area with boulders scattered in patterns at the bottom of a shallow depression.
37.08	59.71	Turn right at a junction with a blue-blazed trail, which forms the western side of the Rock Run Trails System (RRTS) cross-country ski loop. See the separate chapter on the RRTS later in this book. After the turn, follow both the yellow blazes of the AFT and the blue blazes of the RRTS for the next 4.78 mi (7.70 km). The trail is on an old railroad grade through open high-altitude woods.
37.52	60.42	Scramble into and out of a small side hollow. The trail begins a very long and gradual descent, essentially approaching the bottom of the valley in a diagonal fashion.
38.15	61.43	The RRTS Junction Trail (also blue-blazed) descends to the left, crosses a footbridge over the Middle Branch of Rock Run, then leads 0.14 mi (0.22 km) to the east side of the cross-country ski loop. There are some possibilities for camping in this area, especially to the left on the other side of the stream. Meanwhile, the AFT continues straight ahead at this junction, still following the western side of the RRTS loop, and now paralleling the stream. Note the extensive meadows in this valley, which are probably the result of beaver dams in which the critters' ponds gradually filled in with silt, leaving flat and treeless areas. You are likely to see some current beaver ponds as well.
38.34	61.74	A robust spring emerges from under the trail to the left. Water quality is acceptable except during dry periods.
38.69	62.30	Cross a small side stream on logs. Water quality is questionable.
39.06	62.90	As the trail approaches the height of land, the open valley has been left behind. The Middle Branch of Rock Run comes into view again, and here it is a more typical tumbling brook.

MI	KM	DESCRIPTION
39.20	63.12	Off the trail to the left is a nice campsite alongside the run, where good water is available. Next, Upper Rock Run features a series of small waterfalls that are visible from the trail. Watch for muddy seeps along the trail in this area.
39.28	63.25	Footbridge over Upper Rock Run, after which the trail bears right.
39.32	63.32	Turn left and climb briefly over a height of land above Rock Run hollow.
39.50	63.61	Pass a large spring to the left of the trail. Water quality is adequate once it starts flowing.
39.66	63.86	Pass a nice little campsite on the right, just before a footbridge over a spring-fed stream. Water quality is acceptable except during dry periods.
39.83	64.14	Turn right at a junction in the RRTS network. Please sign in at the trail register. (The eastern side of the ski loop goes straight ahead.) The AFT, still combined with a segment of the RRTS, turns right and continues to the south, toward PA 504.
39.99	64.40	Enter an area populated by young evergreens and a lot of ferns. This area was logged about 10–15 years before this writing; to the left you can see a more recent and far more extensive logging zone.
40.42	65.08	A large spring (good water quality when flowing) emerges from under the trail to the right, forming an upper tributary of Benner Run. Note that the AFT has quietly entered a different watershed, as the Rock Run streams flowed to the north and Benner Run is to the west.
40.70	65.54	Another extreme upper tributary of Benner Run appears to the right of the trail. Water quality in this stream is generally acceptable, except during dry periods.

MI	KM	DESCRIPTION
41.01	66.04	Cross a footbridge, then turn left and continue to follow the watercourse upstream. In this area, the run is dry for most of the year, but it can be quite robust during wet periods.
41.08	66.15	Leave the forest and bear right into an extensive fern-filled meadow at the site of an old clearcut. On the far side, encounter artificially planted trees including some Christmas-style spruces. [Seeley, 81] The communications towers visible to the south were built along PA 504 at a high point above the Allegheny Front, to help signals from State College and Bald Eagle Valley reach Western Pennsylvania.
41.16	66.28	After passing under a clutch of Christmas trees, turn left onto a jeep road.
41.35	66.59	Continue straight ahead at a staggered junction with two other grassy jeep roads. Nice meadows are visible off to the right.
41.45	66.75	At a post sign, turn left off the jeep road and onto trail. (Formerly, the RRTS continued straight ahead to Tram Road, and this is now an alternate approach to the parking area on PA 504.)
41.60	66.99	Minor vista to the right, over the upper reaches of Benner Run. On a clear day, the high plateau area around Snow Shoe is visible in the far distance. The highest point on the Allegheny Front Trail is in this area, at 2,531 feet above sea level. [Seeley, 70] The sparse traffic on Rattlesnake Pike (PA 504) can now be heard.
41.70	67.15	Enter a large meadow. Watch the footpath carefully, as there are no trees on which to paint blazes. In the middle of the meadow, continue straight ahead at an intersection with a wide grassy lane. Upon re-entering the woods on the far side, the parking lot on Rattlesnake Pike comes into view.

MI	KM	DESCRIPTION
41.86	67.41	Reach Rattlesnake Pike at the AFT/RRTS parking area. This is the end of the Allegheny Front Trail loop! The AFT continues to the south on the other side of the road, and at the beginning of this chapter.

GUIDE TO THE MOSS-HANNE TRAIL

The guide describes the Moss-Hanne Trail (MHT) in the counter-clockwise direction, from the end of West Side Road in Black Moshannon State Park. For details on reaching this point, see the *Access and Logistics* chapter earlier in this book.

MI	KM	DESCRIPTION
0.00	0.00	From the cul-de-sac at the end of West Side Road, start at the trailhead sign next to the parking spots. This is the beginning of the long-distance Moss-Hanne Trail and the shorter Bog Trail and Indian Trail. There are several tourist trails in this area so watch the signs carefully. Begin by walking through shady hemlocks toward the lake. After just 90 feet, turn right (west) at a junction. (The Bog Trail goes straight ahead.) After the turn, proceed with the lake to your left and a fair number of rocks underfoot.
0.35	0.56	Short plank boardwalk over a wet area.
0.41	0.66	Turn left at a signed trail junction. (A segment of Indian Trail goes right.) The sign gives a distance of 7.3 miles for the Moss-Hanne Trail. That is the distance from this spot to Beaver Road at the southeastern corner of the state park, via the MHT and a shared segment of the Allegheny Front Trail.
0.51	0.82	A short side trail on the left leads down to the lake, with many lily pads within sight.
0.56	0.90	Pass another short side trail on the left. This site is marked by a memorial sign for three people who died when their small plane crashed near here in 1974.

MI	KM	DESCRIPTION
0.60	0.97	Turn left at another signed trail junction. (Another segment of the Indian Trail goes straight ahead.) After the left turn, the MHT heads gently downhill toward an arm of Black Moshannon Lake.
0.64	1.02	Follow a plank boardwalk over a swampy area and a small incoming run.
0.93	1.50	A minor elevation gain of a couple dozen feet leads you into a noticeably different ecosystem of high-altitude trees and shrubs. Next, the trail heads away from the lake and proceeds uneventfully across a gently rolling landscape with a lot of young trees.
0.99	1.60	Mile 1 marker on a short wooden post. There are seven of these on the way to Beaver Road on the far side of the state park. You will notice in this guide to the MHT that the markers do not all fall at precise mile points. This is because of minor rounding errors between your present author and the unknown person who first measured the trail and placed the markers decades ago. Also, due to the need for strategic spots that provide visibility and stability for the posts, some were not quite placed at precise mile points, and may be off by a few dozen feet.
1.71	2.76	Enter a large plantation of red pines, planted near the lake by the Civilian Conservation Corps during the New Deal era.
1.78	2.86	Curve to the right, leaving the pine plantation and entering a more varied forest. Note the sea of ferns underfoot in this area, which indicates a robust local deer population that has an often-deleterious impact on the plant life on the forest floor.
1.98	3.19	Mile 2 marker.
2.29	3.69	After a considerable distance inland, the MHT briefly comes back to within shouting distance of Black Moshannon Lake. Proceed through a forest of young trees with another pine plantation a short distance to the right.

MI	KM	DESCRIPTION
2.47	3.98	The MHT has joined what appears to be an old road grade, which is very grassy and muddy underfoot. The trail then rises briefly to higher ground and dries out.
2.61	4.21	Slosh through a muddy area caused by seep springs.
2.67	4.30	Turn left, cross a footbridge over a muck-filled stream, then keep left again through another muddy area.
2.71	4.37	First of a series of short plank boardwalks.
2.86	4.61	Enter another plantation of very tall pines that were clearly planted in a pattern, with some younger and less organized trees of other species below. For about the next three-quarters of a mile, the MHT weaves in and out of various corners of this plantation several times.
3.00	4.82	Mile 3 marker.
3.32	5.35	Reach the first of two short plank boardwalks, with the second going over a small run (not suitable for drinking). Between the two boardwalks is a very wet area that could use its own boardwalk. You may ask, "Why didn't they just build a continuous boardwalk all the way through?" Unfortunately, it is not that simple, because the wet area may have once been dry before groundwater flow patterns changed, while all of these boardwalks were built from planks that had to be hauled in by hand from far away.
3.55	5.72	Begin a series of longer plank boardwalks over various wet areas.
3.59	5.79	Turn left at a signed trail junction. (Straight ahead the Blueberry Trail, also with boardwalks, heads to a specially cultivated arboretum of native plants within the grounds of Mid State Airport.) After the left turn, the MHT soon meets a solidly constructed beach-style boardwalk, much wider and higher than those seen so far, which constitutes a wooden walkway over an arm of the Black Moshannon wetlands

The beginning of the long boardwalk over the wetland.

MI	KM	DESCRIPTION
(cont.)		This particular boardwalk is about 700 feet long, so please consider the effort required to build it. Thousands of pieces of lumber were hauled in by hand from a lengthy distance, and the boardwalk builders would have had to stand in the swamp during construction.
3.74	6.02	End of the boardwalk, followed by a gentle rise to slightly higher ground.
3.82	6.15	Begin another series of smaller plank boardwalks, with some gaps along the way.
3.92	6.32	Reach a trail junction with a bench. This time, the MHT goes straight ahead, while another segment of the Blueberry Trail heads off to the right.
4.00	6.44	Mile 4 marker.
4.13	6.65	Begin another significant beach-style boardwalk journey across a wide-open stretch of the Black Moshannon wetlands. Note the large shrubs colonizing the swamp around the beginning of this boardwalk. Some areas of

The boardwalk rises to form a bridge over the swampy upper reaches of Black Moshannon Creek.

MI	KM	DESCRIPTION
(cont.)		this boardwalk are being overrun by grasses and sedges growing up between the boards, so watch your footing. This boardwalk may also be slippery when wet, with a mushy swamp floor to either side, so this is not a good area for horseplay.
4.22	6.80	The boardwalk rises in the form of a bridge over Black Moshannon Creek. A little to the south this creek is a modest babbling brook, but here it is just downstream from the point where it widens and supplies this vast wetland complex. The reddish-brown coloration of the water is due to acids released by the unique swamp-loving plants in the area. Downstream from here, those acids combine with others from different types of plants carried by incoming tributaries, and Black Moshannon Creek gradually takes on its namesake color. Around the bridge, note the copious lily pads, which host loudmouthed frogs in the evening and send forth large yellow flowers in June. Meanwhile, the wetlands

MI	KM	DESCRIPTION
(cont.)		around the creek may look like dry meadows, but the thick grasses and shrubs grow out of soil that is under several inches of water for most of the year.
4.24	6.83	End of the boardwalk; proceed into a mature forest. Embark on a gentle climb away from the wetland complex. This climb constitutes the only notable elevation change on the Moss-Hanne Trail, though it is still only about 50 feet up.
4.50	7.25	The trail levels off and joins an old road grade, which comes in from Shirks Road and formerly led to coalmines inside the present state park.
4.96	7.99	Reach the first junction with the Allegheny Front Trail, which comes in from the right and joins the road grade presently being followed by the MHT. This is the 9.26 mi point on the AFT, as seen in that trail's description earlier in this book. Both trails go straight ahead and are concurrent for the next 2.78 mi (4.48 km). The remainder of this description of the Moss-Hanne Trail is identical to miles 6.48 through 9.26 of the Allegheny Front Trail description, except in the opposite direction. Sorry if that is confusing, but there are only so many ways to construct a trail guidebook.
5.00	8.06	Mile 5 marker.
5.04	8.12	At a post sign, turn left onto a narrower trail. (Straight ahead, the grassy lane leads 0.15 mi [0.24 km] to the small parking area at the corner of Shirks and Dug Roads.)
5.21	8.40	Cross a small stream on a footbridge. Water quality is acceptable except during dry periods. Next, enter the first of several red pine plantations.
5.62	9.06	Footbridge over a stream. Next, enter a large wet meadow, with an extensive wetland visible to the left. Patches of sand appear underfoot.

MI	KM	DESCRIPTION
5.73	9.23	As of 2024, there is an enormous beaver pond just to the left of the trail, formed by an impressive dam that is at least 200 feet long. The pond nearly reaches the trail.
5.79	9.33	Enter a large meadow. This one has a variety of both dry and wet plant species.
5.99	9.65	Mile 6 marker. In this area you will traverse a series of narrow plank boardwalks, built by Keystone Trails Association in 2018 in an attempt to rise above the mud.
6.21	10.01	Cross a small meadow filled with unique water-loving grasses and shrubs. The southern end of Black Moshannon Lake, and its bordering swamps and bogs, can be seen through the trees to the left. This area regularly features beaver dams.
6.98	11.25	Mile 7 marker.
7.06	11.38	Cross a stream on logs. The trail is easy and uneventful for about the next half mile.
7.52	12.12	You are walking through a red pine plantation. Note the regular placement and uniform size of most of the trees, plus the general absence of other tree species in the area. The Black Moshannon region was extensively planted with red pine during the development of the state park.
7.55	12.16	Note the unique trees and shrubs in this area, as you are walking along the edge of the wetland. Begin another series of boardwalks that carry the MHT/AFT over many wetland areas that drain into the southern end of Black Moshannon Lake. The boardwalks can be slippery when wet.
7.62	12.28	Traverse the first of several breaks in the boardwalk. Note the patches of soft and springy sphagnum moss along the trail. Watch your footing carefully along the non-boardwalk segments, which are often muddy. [Seeley, 96]

MI	KM	DESCRIPTION
7.68	12.37	The boardwalk rises and forms a bridge over Shirks Run, an unusually deep and fast-flowing stream. This stream features the dark hue that contributes to the distinctive coloration of Black Moshannon Creek downstream.
7.71	12.42	Reach the end of the boardwalks.
7.74	12.47	Reach Beaver Road and the official end of the Moss-Hanne Trail. This is the 6.48 mi point of the Allegheny Front Trail, which has shared its path with the MHT through the southern portions of the state park. The AFT continues eastbound on the other side of the road. Use caution here because of the limited visibility for drivers. Parking at this crossing is not recommended; the parking area at the corner of Strawband Beaver Road is just beyond the curve to the right and is reached via a short side trail encountered by the AFT 0.18 mi (0.29 km) ahead.

GUIDE TO THE SHINGLE MILL TRAIL

The guide describes the Shingle Mill Trail (SMT) in the northbound direction, from its trailhead on Benner Run Road a short distance north of the beach in the center of Black Moshannon State Park. For details on reaching this point, see the *Access and Logistics* chapter earlier in this book.

You will see trail signs that describe the SMT as 3.5 miles long; this is a minor under-estimate, and the trail is actually 3.67 mi (5.91 km). Note that for the first 0.85 mi (1.38 km), the SMT is within the boundaries of the state park, so primitive camping is prohibited along that section of the trail.

MI	KM	DESCRIPTION
0.00	0.00	The SMT begins at a parking area next to Kephart Dam on Black Moshannon Lake, within the boundaries of the state park. From the trail sign at the corner of the parking lot, proceed down a brief gravel path through a grassy area. Watch for the yellow blazes. With the dam on the left, turn right past trees along the embankment. Note that this first segment of the SMT is also included in the Lake Loop Trail.
0.04	0.06	Turn left on the park maintenance road and cross the bridge over Black Moshannon Creek.
0.06	0.10	At the end of the guardrail, turn right onto the yellow-blazed footpath. After this turn, the Shingle Mill Trail follows Black Moshannon Creek northbound, downstream. Note the dark but clear coloration of Black Moshannon Creek, due to decaying plant matter in the wetlands

MI	KM	DESCRIPTION
(cont.)		that feed the southern end of the lake at the state park. The coloration process for the Black Moshannon is natural and is not harmful to the health of the creek. Along Black Moshannon Creek you may also see frothing clumps of what look like dirty soapsuds. These are also the product of the area's unique flora, as decaying plants release botanical oils into the creek. When those oils collect in small whirlpools or corners in the stream, the pressure causes them to lather up into big piles of suds. These are also natural with no harm to the ecosystem. A more complex version of this process is used to make some types of organic soap.
0.10	0.16	Pass a small concrete structure which is part of the state park's water supply system. The SMT is now following Black Moshannon Creek closely. Any water taken from the creek should be treated prior to human consumption, because by this point it has collected many tributaries, and the water has passed through the lake and dam up at the state park.
0.34	0.55	The trail slabs up and around a steep area on the hillside. The SMT will do this a few more times while attempting to hug the edge of Black Moshannon Creek.
0.56	0.90	Cross a side stream (not suitable for drinking), just before an immense old hemlock that hangs over the creek. Note how this tree used to have a second trunk, which appears to have broken off dramatically long ago.
0.64	1.02	Another noteworthy ancient tree hanging over the water—this one an enormous old "wolf" style red oak. (A wolf tree has many large branches near the ground, pointing in all directions, allowing the tree to hog all of the area's sunlight.) Note the flat pool in the creek, behind what's left of an old fisherman's dam.
0.78	1.25	Another brief slab up and around a steep section of the bank.

Black Moshannon Creek, along Shingle Mill Trail, downstream from the dam and lake at Black Moshannon State Park.

MI	KM	DESCRIPTION
0.85	1.38	Cross the unmarked northern boundary of the state park, after which primitive camping is permitted. Next, the trail veers inland a bit.
1.01	1.62	The SMT rejoins Black Moshannon Creek at a huge double-trunked hemlock at the water's edge.
1.07	1.72	Cross a sandy tributary stream (water quality acceptable) on a relatively new footbridge, then climb up a minor ridgeline.
1.24	2.00	Begin a steep and rocky climb up the side of the hollow, after which the SMT stays above the creek for a while.
1.39	2.24	After a rocky descent, rejoin Black Moshannon Creek in a nice hemlock grove, then turn left along the creekside. For the rest of its distance, the SMT has trouble staying along the edge of the creek, veering inland then back again repeatedly. Some of the inland areas feature open meadows. With all these curves along the SMT you can see several different varieties of bottomland ecosystems.

MI	KM	DESCRIPTION
1.68	2.71	Cross a muddy side stream, not suitable for drinking. To the right is a small island in the creek, followed by an especially large artificial pool and the remains of an old splash dam. [Seeley, 98] At the time of writing, beavers had commandeered the old human structure.
1.81	2.91	Cross Huckleberry Road. To the right there are some wide areas where a few cars can park. The SMT continues straight ahead.
1.83	2.95	Cross a spring outlet (water quality acceptable), then bear right. Watch the blazes carefully as you enter an area of dense rhododendron.
1.91	3.07	Cross a more robust spring outlet, with better (in season) water quality, followed shortly by a nice campsite in a hemlock grove off to the right of the trail.
1.97	3.17	The trail veers around a small pond formed by an especially powerful spring, with generally good water quality except around the edges. A sandy spot seen at the bottom of the clear pool shows the spring's discharge point.
2.09	3.37	Enter a copse of red pine and giant rhododendron along the creekside.
2.28	3.67	Cross a spring-fed side stream; water quality acceptable. Next you will pass a couple of small but dry campsites to the left of the trail.
2.48	3.99	Pass through a shrubby meadow that may have been the location of an old building.
2.57	4.14	Step over the remains of a rock wall, which may have been a catchment structure for a spring that still drips from under a hemlock to the left. Water quality is mostly a moot point because this spring drips feebly, even during wet periods.

MI	KM	DESCRIPTION
2.62	4.22	View of the largest artificial pool yet, at the site of an old clay mining operation. Beavers have been known to use the old stone dam as a foundation for their own construction projects. Legend has it that this pool can get as much as 13 feet deep. Next, the trail turns left into an especially rocky area.
3.08	4.96	Reach Split Rock, a large, flat boulder that juts out into the creek. This is a nice spot for a break. A large chunk of the boulder has broken off into the channel. There are some natural rapids as the creek turns a corner, though there is a flat pool formed by another old fisherman's dam just downstream from the boulder.
3.30	5.32	Climb gently through a rocky, fern-filled meadow. The SMT begins to trend above and away from Black Moshannon Creek. When the leaves are down, you can see a large island in the creek.
3.65	5.88	Emerge at the top of a steep embankment above a side channel of Black Moshannon Creek. The segment of the creek visible far below and to the right is often the site of beaver activity.
3.67	5.91	Reach the northern end of the Shingle Mill Trail, at the 31.39 mi point on the Allegheny Front Trail. Here the AFT goes to the left (westbound) or straight ahead (eastbound). Please sign in at the trail register.

GUIDE TO THE ROCK RUN TRAILS SYSTEM

Starting at its 37.08 mi point, the Allegheny Front Trail shares its path with part of the Rock Run Trails System (RRTS). This RRTS network was designed for cross-country skiing, and also offers a delightful hiking experience during the off season. The trails in the system follow several old railroad grades, some with significant historical interest, and offer mostly level or gently sloping travel along various branches of Rock Run.

The RRTS consists of a long two-way entrance trail and a loop that can be completed in one direction. The total distance traversed in this fashion is 12.15 miles. The loop can also be shortened via a cross-connector trail for a total distance of 7.54 miles. The RRTS network was constructed specifically for skiers in the early 1980s by the Penn State Outing Club, under the direction of the intrepid Ralph Seeley and Tom Thwaites.

The construction of this network inspired grand ideas for the Allegheny Front Trail, but the RRTS was a stand-alone entity until the late 1990s, when the AFT finally reached the area. The AFT now utilizes a portion of the western side of the RRTS loop and the entire entrance trail.

In general, hikers are encouraged to use cross-country ski trails during the non-winter months, to cut down on undergrowth and to keep the pathway distinct. But anyone who hikes these trails in the winter must make amends for cross-country skiers, for whom the RRTS network was designated. Cross-country enthusiasts will hit these trails in droves as soon as there are more than about six inches of snow on the ground. Hikers who walk the trails when snow is present are likely to leave "postholes"—the term for cavernous footprints in the deep snow. Postholes are a nuisance and even a hazard for skiers.

Winter hikers should make every effort to avoid leaving postholes on these trails. This can be accomplished by wearing snowshoes. When those are not available, walk to the side of the trail so your footprints are off the main pathway. The cross-country skiing season in Pennsylvania is usually very short, so that sport's enthusiasts should be allowed to enjoy their designated trails with a minimum of distractions. [Seeley, 68-69]

HIKING OPTIONS

- The entire RRTS system, including the full loop and the entrance trail in both directions (as described below), results in a hike of 12.15 miles (19.57 km).
- For a shorter hike that skips the northern segments of the RRTS system: Follow the entrance trail for 2.03 miles, the east side of RRTS loop for 1.66 miles to the Junction Trail intersection, the Junction Trail westbound for 0.14 mile, the west side of RRTS for 1.68 miles to the intersection with the entrance trail, and the entrance trail in opposite direction for 2.03 miles. This results in a hike of 7.54 miles (12.14 km).

This description of the RRTS begins at the trailhead parking lot that is shared by the Allegheny Front Trail and the Rock Run Trails System. The description begins in the northbound direction from this starting point (see the *Access and Logistics* chapter of this book for more details). Note that the RRTS is marked with blue blazes, and the segments shared with the AFT are marked with blazes that are blue and yellow.

MI	KM	DESCRIPTION
0.00	0.00	The first segment of the RRTS (originally known as the entrance trail) is concurrent with the Allegheny Front Trail, corresponding to the 39.83 to 41.86 mi points in the AFT description earlier in this book but in the opposite direction. Sorry if that is confusing, but there are only so many ways to construct a trail guidebook. To begin the RRTS as described here, start at the AFT/RRTS parking area at the corner of Rattlesnake Pike and Tram Road. Head north, following the combined blue/yellow blazes, and proceed through a brief wooded zone followed by a large meadow.

MI	KM	DESCRIPTION
0.26	0.42	Minor vista to the left, over the upper reaches of Benner Run. On a clear day, the high plateau area around Snow Shoe is visible in the far distance. The highest point in the Allegheny Front Trail network is in this area, at 2,531 feet elevation above sea level. [Seeley, 70]
0.41	0.66	At a post sign, turn right onto a jeep road and head downhill.
0.51	0.82	Continue straight ahead at a staggered junction with two other grassy jeep roads. Nice meadows are visible off to the left.
0.70	1.13	Turn right off of the jeep road and onto a narrower trail. Pass through an extensive fern-filled meadow at the site of an old clearcut, with artificially planted trees including some Christmas-style spruces. [Seeley, 81] The communications towers visible to the south were built along PA 504 at a high point above the Allegheny Front, to help signals from State College and Bald Eagle Valley reach Western Pennsylvania.
0.78	1.26	The trail curves broadly to the left and reenters the forest. An upper tributary of Benner Run (usually dry) appears alongside the trail.
0.85	1.37	Cross a footbridge, then continue to follow the watercourse downstream. At this spot, the run is dry for most of the year, but it can be quite robust during wet periods.
1.16	1.87	In this area the stream alongside the trail may now be flowing. Water quality is generally acceptable, except during dry periods.
1.44	2.33	A large spring (good water quality when flowing) emerges from under the trail to the left, forming another upper tributary of Benner Run.
1.87	3.01	Enter an area populated by young evergreens and a lot of ferns. This area was logged about 10-15 years before this writing; to the right you can see a more recent and far more extensive logging zone.

MI	KM	DESCRIPTION
2.03	3.27	Turn right at a junction in the RRTS network. Please sign in at the trail register. The Allegheny Front Trail departs to the left and takes one side of the RRTS loop with it. To continue on the RRTS as described here (counter-clockwise), turn right onto the eastern side of the loop. Follow the blue-only blazes after the right turn. The trail rises gently at first, then gets steeper a little later.
2.20	3.54	Pass an old Rock Run Trails sign, then cross an old forestry road and continue through a sparse hilltop forest. The road crossing is at an odd angle, so watch blazes carefully. Next, pass another trail sign that denotes the older ski trails (Headwaters, Woodland) that were incorporated into the RRTS in the 1980s.
2.25	3.63	Begin a very long and gradual descent into the valley of Rock Run.
2.60	4.19	Pass through a clutch of large boulders, still descending. Watch for a sharp right turn.
2.71	4.36	Cross a minor watercourse, still descending gradually.
2.88	4.65	Cross another minor run, then turn left onto an elevated old railroad grade, still descending.
3.24	5.22	The trail has levelled off on another old railroad grade, parallel to and slightly above the bottom of the valley, which is to your left.
3.29	5.30	Plunge into a deep but usually dry streambed and then climb back out. There are several more such trenches ahead. These trenches are probably the result of old clear-cutting practices during the logging era, when the forest was uniformly denuded. With no trees to absorb rainfall, severe storms formed rampaging streams that dug deep trenches into the landscape. Now that the forest has regrown, these deep trenches might carry feeble and seasonal streams, but they are usually dry, with little impact except annoyance for hikers and skiers.

MI	KM	DESCRIPTION
3.69	5.94	Reach an intersection with the Junction Trail, which heads to the left. Note that a sign at this intersection under-measures the distance you have hiked so far from PA 504. See the sidebar below. To continue on the main RRTS loop, turn right (north).

SIDEBAR: JUNCTION TRAIL

When hiking westbound from the intersection described in the entry above, the Junction Trail descends easily through a brushy and rocky meadow. At the bottom it passes through a nice camping area along both sides of the Middle Branch of Rock Run. The Junction Trail crosses a footbridge over the run then rises briefly to the trail that makes up the west side of the RRTS, which at that spot is still multiplexed with the AFT. That is the 8.44 mi point in the RRTS loop as described later in this chapter. The total length of the Junction Trail is 0.14 mi (0.22 km).

BACK ON THE MAIN RRTS LOOP

MI	KM	DESCRIPTION
3.78	6.09	Head north after the intersection with the Junction Trail. Go up a brief rise and then turn left on a well-defined old railroad grade that remains on a bench slightly above the bottom of the valley. A short distance ahead, as of 2024 you can see a very large beaver pond in the Middle Branch of Rock Run to your left. You will also notice some large springs in this area, at the bottom of the elevated grade you are following.
4.28	6.89	Hop across a rocky run that carries a stripe of rhododendron through the woods. Questionable water quality.
4.34	6.99	Pass the remains of a rock retaining wall, which would have propped up the old railroad through a soggy area.

A large beaver pond in the Middle Branch of Rock Run, as seen at the time of writing.

MI	KM	DESCRIPTION
4.57	7.36	The trail curves broadly to the northwest, as the formerly wide Rock Run valley closes in on all sides. In this area you will see more evidence of the former railroad track's solid construction, with retaining walls and embankments built by hand with the local rocks.
4.97	8.00	Enter a crowded area of evergreens and giant rhododendron bushes, indicating a transition into a wetter sub-ecosystem.
5.05	8.13	Cross a small run; questionable water quality.
5.23	8.42	You find yourself on a very rocky grade that was built above the natural forest floor, to keep the old railroad level and protect it from flooding. The boisterous Middle Branch of Rock Run is audible somewhere to your left. Note the abrupt change in the understory, between rhododendron (wet) to your left and mountain laurel (dry) to your right.

MI	KM	DESCRIPTION
5.30	8.54	The solid old rocky railroad ends abruptly, and the trail continues straight ahead, downhill. This was most likely the eastern end of a long wooden trestle bridge that carried trains over the creek. That bridge, and many others in the area, would have been dismantled, or collapsed and washed away, decades ago. [Seeley, 71]
5.33	8.58	Turn left and cross the high, sturdy footbridge over the Middle Branch of Rock Run, in an especially scenic spot. This bridge was built in the late 2010s to replace an older and skinnier one that was both wobbly and extra tough for cross-country skiers. At the far end of the bridge, the trail turns right and enters a jungle of rhododendron. Meanwhile, be suspicious of the water quality in the creek, because (as you may have already seen), its upper valley is often dammed by beavers, and this alters natural filtration processes.
5.41	8.71	After diverging from the creek a bit, the trail joins another rocky old railroad grade, which is probably a continuation of the same track at the other end of the long-gone trestle bridge.
5.72	9.22	Footbridge over the West Branch of Rock Run; acceptable water quality. The trail then curves to the north, as the old railroad followed the contours of the hollow.
5.88	9.46	Note the old rock wall just uphill to your left. You will walk along its top a few minutes from now.
5.96	9.59	Make a very sharp U-turn to the left (south) at a junction of old railroad grades. You are joining a different old track that used to take logging trains, and now you, on a long and slanted journey up the side of the hollow above the Rock Run watershed.
6.35	10.23	The West Branch of Rock Run becomes visible downhill to your left, in a great camping area if you choose to scramble down there.

MI	KM	DESCRIPTION
6.42	10.33	Watch carefully for a surprise switchback to the right (north), continuing to follow the old grade uphill. You have missed this turn if you find yourself at the edge of the West Branch of Rock Run. Here, the old railroad track made a sharp turn to the right to continue up the hillside, but there appears to have been an open area ahead where trains (or the horses that pulled them) switched to reverse gear before heading up the next segment. This turn-around area can cause confusion for today's hikers and skiers, though it may also be a nice campsite.
6.45	10.39	Switchback sharply to the left (south) at another junction of old railroad grades. After this turn, you will see some possible camping spots along the run, downhill to your left.
6.83	11.00	Watch carefully for a surprise left turn, off the obvious old railroad grade you've been following and onto a much narrower footpath. You soon cross another footbridge over the West Branch of Rock Run; acceptable water quality. After the bridge, the trail climbs moderately to the top of the plateau.
7.15	11.51	The trail has levelled off in a thin hilltop forest.
7.37	11.87	Reach a junction with the Allegheny Front Trail, which comes in from the right. Straight ahead, the two trails share the same path for the rest of their respective distances to PA 504. Note the yellow/blue blazes. The remainder of this description of the RRTS corresponds to that for the AFT earlier in this book, between its 37.08 and 41.86 mi points.
7.81	12.58	Scramble into and out of a small side hollow. The trail begins a very long and gradual descent, essentially approaching the bottom of the valley in a diagonal fashion.

MI	KM	DESCRIPTION
8.44	13.59	The RRTS Junction Trail (also blue-blazed) descends to the left, crosses a footbridge over the Middle Branch of Rock Run, then leads 0.14 mi (0.22 km) to the east side of the cross-country ski loop. There are some possibilities for camping in this area, especially to the left on the other side of the stream. Meanwhile, the RRTS main loop continues straight ahead at this junction, now paralleling the stream. Note the extensive meadows in this valley, which are probably the result of beaver dams in which the critters' ponds gradually filled in with silt, leaving flat and treeless areas. You will probably see some current beaver ponds as well.
8.63	13.90	A robust spring emerges from under the trail to the left. Water quality is acceptable except during dry periods.
8.98	14.46	Cross a small side stream on logs. Water quality is questionable.

The Junction Trail's footbridge over the Middle Branch of Rock Run.

MI	KM	DESCRIPTION
9.35	15.06	As the trail approaches the height of land, the open valley has been left behind. The Middle Branch of Rock Run comes into view again, and here it is a more typical tumbling brook.
9.49	15.28	Off the trail to the left is a nice campsite alongside the run, where good water is available. Next, Upper Rock Run features a series of small waterfalls that are visible from the trail. Watch for a few muddy seeps along the trail in this area.
9.57	15.41	Footbridge over Upper Rock Run, after which the trail bears right.
9.61	15.48	Turn left and climb briefly over a height of land above Rock Run hollow.
9.79	15.77	Pass a large spring to the left of the trail. Water quality is adequate once it starts flowing.
9.95	16.02	Pass a nice little campsite on the right, just before a footbridge over a spring-fed stream. Water quality is acceptable except during dry periods.
10.12	16.30	Turn right at a junction in the RRTS network. Please sign in at the trail register. (Ahead is the eastern side of the ski loop, which you have already done.) The RRTS turns right, still sharing its path with the AFT, and heads south toward PA 504. If you are completing the RRTS as described in this chapter, you have already experienced the points below but in the opposite direction. The text has been simplified for brevity.
10.71	17.24	A large spring (good water quality when flowing) emerges from under the trail to the right, forming an upper tributary of Benner Run.
11.30	18.20	Cross a footbridge, then turn left and continue to follow a usually dry watercourse upstream.
11.37	18.31	Leave the forest and bear right into an extensive fern-filled meadow at the site of an old clearcut.

MI	KM	DESCRIPTION
11.45	18.44	After passing under a clutch of evergreens, turn left onto a jeep road.
11.74	18.91	At a post sign, turn left off the jeep road and onto trail.
11.99	19.31	Enter a large meadow. Watch the footpath carefully, as there are no trees on which to paint blazes. In the middle of the meadow, continue straight ahead at an intersection with a wide grassy lane. Upon re-entering the woods on the far side, the parking lot on Rattlesnake Pike comes into view.
12.15	19.57	Reach Rattlesnake Pike at the AFT/RRTS parking area. This is the end of the Rock Run Trails System. Note that the Allegheny Front Trail continues on the other side of the road.

ABOUT THE AUTHOR

Ben Cramer has hiked more than 6,000 miles on Pennsylvania's hiking trails and has completed many of the state's long-distance backpacking trails multiple times. He is a longtime member of Keystone Trails Association and was a member of its board of directors from 2018 to 2023. He is also a member of several Pennsylvania conservation groups and hiking clubs; and was formerly an executive committee member for Sierra Club at both the local and state levels.

Cramer is the author of seven guidebooks for Pennsylvania backpacking trails, including two previous editions for the *Allegheny Front Trail*. With one exception, none of those long-distance trails had dedicated guidebooks previously. Cramer was also the editor of *Pennsylvania Hiking Trails* (13th edition, 2008). For several years he wrote regularly on outdoor adventure and environmental issues for the *Centre Daily Times*, and for a variety of Pennsylvania volunteer publications.

Under his professional name Benjamin W. Cramer, he is the author of the book *Freedom of Environmental Information* (2011). He is a longtime resident of State College, PA and teaches for the Donald P. Bellisario College of Communications at Penn State University, where one of his research specialties is the environmental impacts of modern telecommunications services.

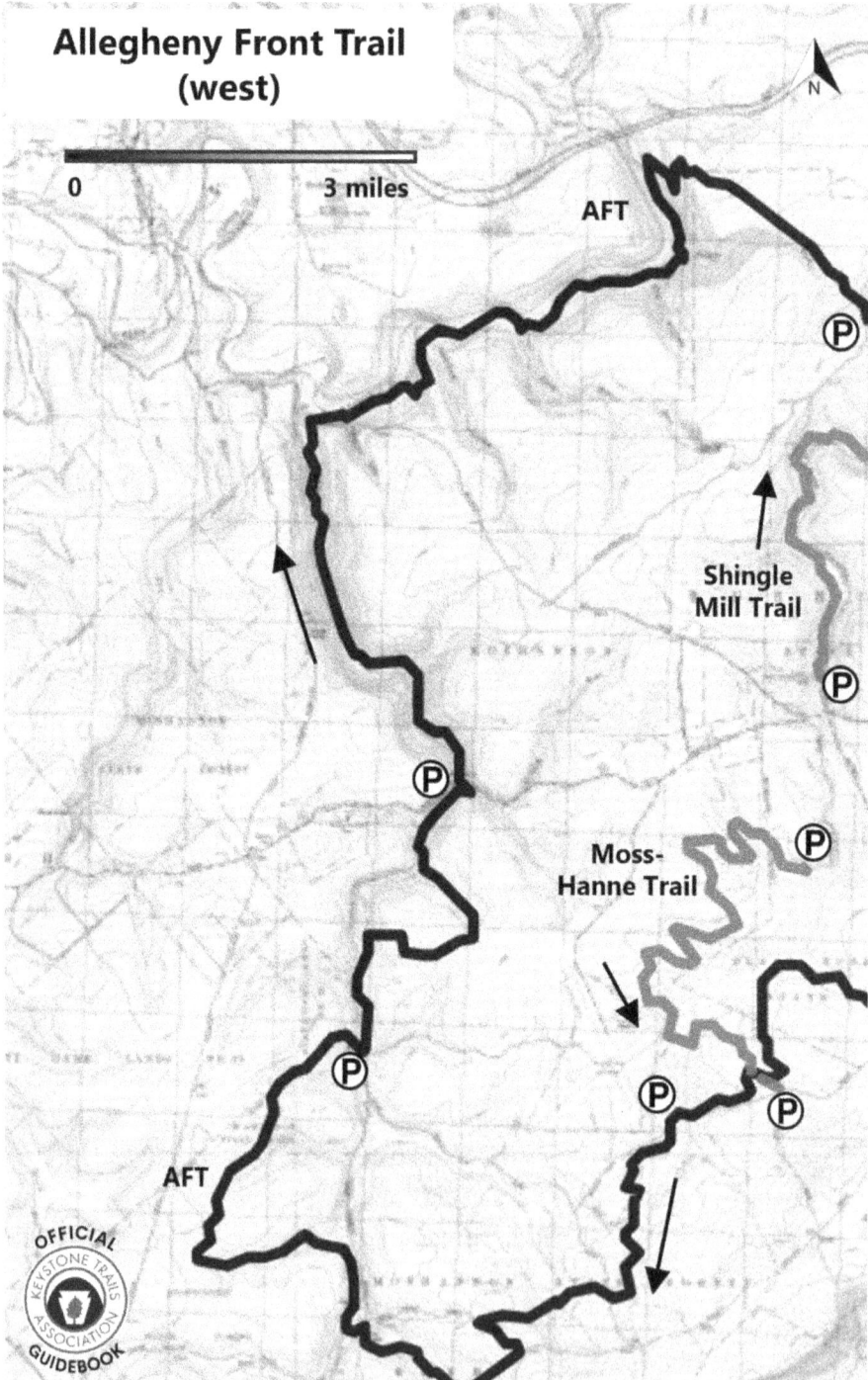

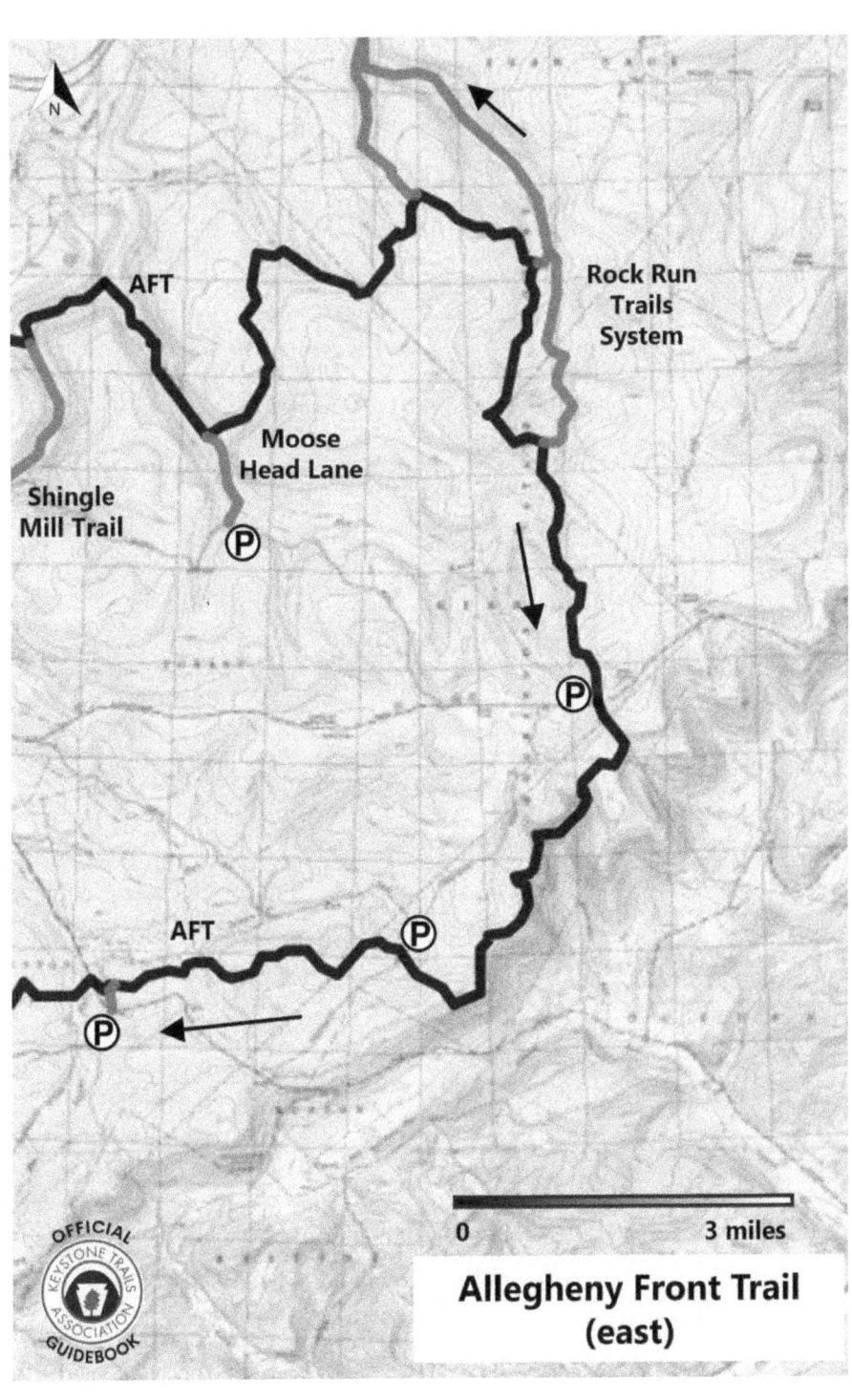

For a larger online map of the Allegheny Front Trail,
visit Keystone Trails Association at:

www.kta-hike.org/maps

or scan here:

These maps illustrate GPS data collected by the author. The online map is courtesy of CalTopo. The printed map on the previous two pages was created with GPS Visualizer, founded and operated by Adam Schneider, with USGS (United States Geologic Survey) maps as the backgrounds. All maps and data are verified for accuracy by the author and Keystone Trails Association.

www.ingramcontent.com/pod-product-compliance
Lightning Source LLC
Chambersburg PA
CBHW031654040426
42453CB00006B/303